FOR THE LORD OF THE ANIMALS— POEMS FROM THE TELUGU

FOR THE LORD OF THE ANIMALS— POEMS FROM THE TELUGU

The *Kāḷahastīśvara Śatakamu* of Dhūrjaṭi

Translated, with
an Introduction and Notes, by
HANK HEIFETZ and
VELCHERU NARAYANA RAO

Afterword by
Velcheru Narayana Rao

UNIVERSITY OF CALIFORNIA PRESS
Berkeley Los Angeles London

University of California Press
Berkeley and Los Angeles, California

University of California Press, Ltd.
London, England

1 2 3 4 5 6 7 8 9

Library of Congress Cataloging in Publication Data

Dhūrjaṭi, 16th cent.
For the Lord of the Animals; poems from the Telugu.

Translation of: Kāḷahastīśvara śatakamu.
1. Siva (Hindu deity)—Poetry. I. Heifetz, Hank.
II. Nārāyaṇarāvu, Vēlcēru, 1932–
III. Title
PL478.9.D6K313 1987 894'.82712 86–6920
ISBN 0–520–05669–8

For my father, Velcheru Buchi Narasinga Rao

For my children, Aaron and Mara Heifetz

Contents

On the Process of Translation ix

Acknowledgments xi

Introduction 1

FOR THE LORD OF THE ANIMALS 13

Notes to the Poems 123

Afterword 131

A Note on Telugu Meter 167

A Note on the Text 169

Transliteration of Telugu and Sanskrit 175

On the Process of Translation

These translations are the product of a collaboration between an American writer who has formally studied other Indian languages but not Telugu and a Telugu writer and scholar for whom some of these poems were recited in childhood, chanted by his father, a learned brahmin in a remote village where the way of life, in many ways, differed little from that of the period in which the poems were composed.

Our method brought us close to the oral tradition—of direct recitation and response—which still, despite the advent of print, exists very strongly as a feature of classical and popular Indian culture. V. Narayana Rao would write out these poems in Telugu, chant them in the traditional style, and supply the literal English meanings. Hank Heifetz would then compose an English poetic version. We would discuss this result, with Narayana Rao drawing on his memory—the true library of the classical Indian scholar—for illuminations and precisions.

Explications of specific words would often open out into whole areas of the Telugu past. Phrases would be changed or emphases altered, as we entered more deeply into the meaning of the poems until finally—for the best of them at least—the translation would reach a form, exhilarating us both, that seemed adequately to represent the original. Small changes might come up later, in private, but much of the work was done "publicly," by word of mouth, linking the process, for us, of contemporary translation to the archaic and fundamental learning mode of face-to-face human dialogue.

Acknowledgments

We should like to thank David Shulman for his scholarly and literary responses, A. K. Ramanujan for his encouragement and for a suggestion in Poem 8, Frances Wilson for her continual interest in our project while we were working together at the University of Wisconsin in Madison, and especially George Hart, who read through an early version of these translations and made a number of helpful suggestions.

We are also grateful to G. Madanamohana Rao of Andhra Pradesh for sending us some additional poems from the Ārya Mudraṇālayamu edition published in India.

Introduction

The temple at Kāḷahasti, a small town in the far south of the modern Indian state of Andhra Pradesh, is built on the bank of a river now known as the Mogileru but in tradition given the Sanskrit name, Suvarṇamukhari, "the River with the Golden Sound." The temple is dedicated to Śrīkāḷahastīśvara, a local manifestation of the god Shiva, and is a revered pilgrimage site for the Telugu-speaking people who are the majority population of the state. It is now about an hour's bus ride—across flat country which turns burning hot in the summer—from the famous and grandiose pilgrimage temple of Tirupati, the Lourdes of South India. Kāḷahasti, in contrast, is a quieter place, more remote, and when it fills up at the time of an important festival (above all on Mahāśivarātri, the Great Night of Shiva, which falls in February or March), the pilgrims are mostly farming people from the local countryside. The temple is built on a slight rise and a shrine within the walls—dedicated to the hunter Kannappa who gave his eyes to the god—is located on a small hill which overlooks a considerable distance. The walls themselves are massive, as befits the palace of the god and perhaps, at one time, the needs of defence for the temple. The site, with its moderate elevation, is a natural place for a fortress overseeing the surrounding plains.

The foundation legend of Kāḷahasti concerns the efforts of three animals—two of them in direct rivalry—to revere the god Shiva, with apparently fatal but eventually exalted results for themselves. The three animals are *śrī*, the spider; *kāḷa*, the snake; and *hasti*, the elephant. (This interpretation of the place name seems to be a "folk etymology," since "Kāḷahasti" is probably a Sanskritizing of "Kāḷatti," the ancient Dravidian name of the site.) The spider worships Shiva by using his webs to decorate a lingam—the phallus-shaped emblem of Shiva—which has appeared in the forest. Shiva tests him by permitting the webs to catch fire from a votive lamp. The spider hurls himself on the fire and tries to swallow it. With the spider at the point of death, Shiva intervenes and bestows upon him that permanent presence in the heaven of Shiva which is Shaivite liberation.

The snake and the elephant cross each other's paths. A snake in Indian legend and literature is always, unless otherwise indicated, a cobra and, according to myth, the cobra grows jewels in his hood. With these jewels, the snake decorates the lingam. The snake does this repeatedly and, once he has left, an elephant repeatedly sweeps aside the jewels with his trunk and bathes the lingam with water, after which he offers flowers, leaves, and lotus stems. Each, ignorant of who the other may be, feels his own process of worship is being assaulted, and on the night of Mahāśivarātri the snake lies in wait, while the elephant has also resolved to deal with his enemy. The battle that follows is characterized by the extreme violence that forms part of many Shaivite devotional legends. The snake enters the elephant's trunk, and the elephant, crazed by the venom, smashes his head against a hill, killing both himself and the cobra. Shiva then appears and takes them both into his heaven.

A subsidiary legend, of almost equal importance and with the same violent tone, is that of the tribal hunter Tinnaḍu, who, after his act of devotion, becomes known as Kannappa, "the Man of the Eyes." He is a tribesman, therefore outside and below the caste system, and worships the lingam with offerings that are ritually polluted by his touch or even, given the tenets of brahminical tradition, in themselves—meat, for instance, or toddy. A brahmin who is also worshiping the lingam objects to the actions of the tribesman. Shiva—to test and demonstrate the intensity of the hunter's devotion—causes an eye on the lingam, perhaps sculpted or painted there, to water as if it were diseased. The tribal tears out one of his own eyes to replace it and then repeats the act when the other eye of the lingam begins to water. Shiva then takes the tribesman to himself.

At some time in the sixteenth century, perhaps while the kings of Vijayanagar, the last great Hindu empire, were still flourishing in Andhra, the poet Dhūrjaṭi came to this temple. He is definitely known, through a colophon, to be the author of the *Kāḷahastīśvara Māhātmyamu* ("Sacred Legends of the Lord of Kāḷahasti"), a long, ornate poem (in the *kāvya* style derived from Sanskrit) which glorifies the temple of Kāḷahasti through an elaborate presentation of the above and other legends. A different sort of work, the *Kāḷahastīśvara Śatakamu*, a collection of short poems directed to the god of the shrine, is strongly attributed, by Telugu tradition, to Dhūrjaṭi as well. Outside of what is evident in the works themselves, almost no definite information exists about his life. We are not even certain that the name Dhūrjaṭi—unusual in the Telugu country—was given to him at birth, since it is an appellation of Shiva—"He Who Has a Weight of Matted Hair"—and the poet may have taken or used it in honor of the god. Legend counts him as one of the Eight Elephants of the Directions, the *aṣṭadiggajas*, a name from classical mythology applied to eight great poets who are supposed to have served at the court of Krishnadevarāya (1509–1529), greatest of the Vijayanagar kings and a famous patron of literature. Neither the existence of this group nor Dhūrjaṭi's membership in it seems anything more than legend. We do know, from his work and his own words in the colophon to his long, ornate poem, that he was a strongly sectarian Shaivite, a *bhaviparāṅmukha*, "opposed to those who are reborn" (because they follow gods other than Shiva), and that his mother was named Siṅgama Ramā Nārāyaṇa, his father Jakkaya Nārāyaṇa, names which suggest (though they do not necessarily prove) a Vaishnavite lineage, raising the possibility that Dhūrjaṭi may at some time have become a convert to Shaivism. He does not give his caste or any further family background, a characteristic of militant Shaivism, whose adherents rejected the formal, rigorously defining affiliations of Hindu kinship and considered themselves born directly into the lineage of Shiva. As to his date, we can say that he probably lived in the middle or latter part of the sixteenth century, because of a reference to him by the poet Veṅkaṭarāya, who lived around 1630, and, perhaps more significantly, by the importance he assigns to the poet, the craft of poetry, and the significance of the relationship between poet and patron—all features most characteristically developed for Telugu letters during the sixteenth century, the height of classical literary production and of Andhra political prominence.

What follows is a translation of nearly the entire *Kāḷahastīśvara Śatakamu*,* as it is known and chanted today among Telugu-speaking people. *Śatakamu* literally means an anthology of a hundred poems, but the number included in such a collection is usually somewhat greater, the auspicious number of 108 being especially favored. The work has never been critically edited, and editions vary as to the exact number of poems and sometimes in specific textual details. Taking various editions into account, we have omitted a small number of poems because they

*Our rendering of the *Kāḷahastīśvara Śatakamu* is the first translation of this work (or of any classical Telugu text) into expressive English. Attempts have been made in Andhra to produce English versions. Though these translators have shown considerable energy and a genuine love for Telugu literature, their translations lack literary value. Works of this kind are Bulusu Venkata Subbarao, *The Voice of Dhurjati* (Visakhapatnam: Andhra University Press, 1977), and Pisipati Krishnamurti, *Śrīkāḷahastīśvara Śatakamu Ānglānuvādamu* (bilingual edition; Hyderabad, published by the author, 1973).

are merely slight variations on poems we have included, because the text is too corrupt for a clear translation, or because they depend on references which are not translatable.

Telugu scholars have tried to construct an imaginary biography for Dhūrjaṭi based on the poems of this collection. Setting aside so speculative an effort, what we can say is that the anthology does seem to embody an emotional biography. Many of the poems—even those which handle rather conventional themes—show the deep imprint of personal experience in the quality of their imagery and the intensity of their feeling. In form, all the poems are statements, exhortations, or appeals to the god of the shrine at Kāḷahasti. As such, they come under the category of *bhakti*, or devotional poetry. At its best, the bhakti poem is the closest thing in classical Indian literary tradition to the Western personal lyric, in contrast to more rigidly prescribed forms such as *kāvya*, the ornate epic (really an extended depersonalized lyric narrative) which can, in the hands of a great poet like the Sanskrit writer Kālidāsa, also communicate deeply felt emotion, but abstracted, aestheticized, consciously universalized. Such a formalized aesthetic approach discourages realism. The bhakti approach encourages it. Released from the formal restraints involved in producing poetry for the courts, Dhūrjaṭi is free to fill his poems with the real world, with personal, social, and contemporary concerns. He communicates directly with a god who is also a sort of beloved relative, at the same time distant and intimate, both overlord and friend, someone to whom he can speak and also in whose name he can really speak to himself.

Most of these poems include or suggest some praise of the god, but the discourse underlying the praise is used for many different purposes, among them psychological and philosophical reflections which include a number of meditations on sensuality—poems that could only have been written by a man of powerful emotions, who does not dismiss passion in a reflex of ascetic automatism but questions and probes and reflects on the experience of his life:

We all take pleasure in seeing
and smelling and hearing and tasting
and the touch of skin pressing against skin.
Why have you made us with these senses
if our using them is a sin?
What do you gain, O God of Kāḷahasti,
by playing this game of illusions
for your own amusement
to while away the time? (Poem 67)

The poems often record his fluctuating moods, including the dark fear of death and, for the Shaivite believer, grim birth after birth:

When I look at myself,
when I think of my actions,
terror descends upon me and
darkness falls across time. (Poem 73)

He can also use the form for subjects less narrowly linked to the most essential limits of the human condition. Some of these poems are statements on aesthetics which elevate the directness of devotional poetry—the poetry of the temple—above the formalized rhetoric of court poetry. The Dhūrjaṭi of our text is clearly a learned man and—if the same poet did write the *Kāḷahastīśvara Māhātmyamu*—himself the author of a poem with devotional content but nevertheless in the highly elaborate style of the royal courts. In this collection as well there are some moments of elaborateness. The aesthetic comments, however, affirm a clear stylistic choice, which is also ideological in that it involves a rejection of the formal apparatus of institutionalized court poetry:

How can you be praised in elaborate language,
similes, conceits, overtones, secondary meanings,
or textures of sound? They cannot contain
your form. Enough of them!
More than enough. Can poetry hold out
before the face of truth? (Poem 49)

and the devotional reasons for the style combine with the aesthetic:

I never think of asking you to give me things,
so if you don't care for my poetry
I'll bear that all right.
It's only my tongue's natural work,
nothing other than my worship. (Poem 62)

Of great interest is the fact that he is a social poet, in some sense a "political" poet, an ancestor of the powerful strain in Telugu literature of socially conscious, socially committed writing. In praising the poet who directs his work toward a god and uses his poetry for self-examination with the intent of self-liberation, Dhūrjaṭi—with the clear tones of bitter experience—attacks institutionalized authority for its ideological pressures, its demands for family life and for sons, and in its human embodiment as the arrogant guru, or the learned man who seeks success at the feet of power, or, most often and repeatedly, power itself in its dress of his time—the person of the king:

If you call a man a king, must he then
say good-by to compassion,
charity, self-respect?

. . . . .

Is there a reason why kings seem to be
a growth from the worst seed?   (Poem 37)

His hatred for kings is contrasted with his devotion to Shiva, but it shows a degree of disgust that is surely a reflection of his reaction to injustice itself:

The very word "King"
so sickens me,
I will never accept it
for myself ever, even
in some other life.   (Poem 22)

These poems, which address a god while dealing with many aspects of the human life cycle and condition, have long been used in the Telugu country, among those who know them by heart, as means of focusing on their own emotions, in time of confusion, trouble, or joy. They are poems which, through the intensity of their expression, have earned a status that is not merely literary; they have themselves taken part in countless lives.

All these poems consist of four-line stanzas in long classical meters, each line of a set of four having the same number of syllables and metrical pattern. If it were the tradition in Telugu to chant these poems with the line as the basic unit of presentation, each poem in performance would have the regular cantilened quality of a verse in Sanskrit—the Indo-European language which is the source of an enormous amount of Telugu vocabulary—or of verse in Tamil, the oldest in literary development among the Dravidian languages, to which group Telugu belongs. Instead, it is the custom in Telugu to chant the poems according to semantic units, so that poems which have the same overall meter may be presented, according to their content, with a very different spacing of elements and general rhythm. To read a poem merely by meter is considered to be reading "like a child." Taking account, then, of how the poems are generally heard and felt in Telugu, we have translated these poems by meaning units, attempting to catch the flow of feeling rather than the formal metrical order. As a result, the lengths of the translations vary considerably, though in Telugu all the poems, in syllabic count, are very close to the same length.

There is another factor which also affects their length in translation. Telugu—especially in this period of its richest literary production—assimilated from Sanskrit not only a vast amount of vocabulary but also the Sanskrit grammatical practice of using long compounds—formed of nouns and modifiers—through which considerable information could be crowded into a brief space. Using this method, the poet could create rather intricate poems within the same metrical limitations as simpler poems consisting mostly of pure Telugu words. These Sanskritic nominal compounds break down naturally into phrases in English and produce longer, more elaborate poems that are analogues of their structure in Telugu. Another very interesting aspect of the mixed Sanskrit and Telugu vocabulary is that Sanskrit words, like Latinate vocabulary in English, tend to be used for relatively formal, elevated speech while the Telugu vocabulary—often in the same poems and for specific shifts of tone—will be used for very direct, even colloquial statements of feeling, just as Anglo-Saxon words are frequently used for the same purposes in English. We have tried, where possible, to convey some of this sense of changing tones.

Each of the poems in Telugu has the formal ending *śrīkāḷahastīśvarā*, a vocative which, very literally translated, means "Lord of the Spider, the Snake, and the Elephant!" *Kāḷa* and *hasti* clearly mean "snake" and "elephant." The word *śrī*, in its ordinary usage, is an honorific title prefixed to a name as a mark of respect. According to tradition, it refers, in this compound only, to the spider. For the Telugu reader or listener, the phrase provides an expected musical completion for the poem and is felt as a reference and address to the god of the shrine at Kāḷahasti, not as a continuous recall of the foundation legends which, etymologically, it expresses. There are two problems in translating a fixed phrase like this one—the issues of literalness and of position in the verse. Given that the quality of the phrase when translated barely and literally into English calls a great deal of somewhat bizarre attention to itself—and this sort of stress is not warranted at all by its actual function in the poems—we have decided to translate according to its normally felt meaning, "God of Kālahasti," the resident deity of the shrine. In translation, we have varied the placing of this vocative. It will often be found in its Telugu final position but we have also set it elsewhere, according to its usefulness in the rhythmic expression of the individual poem, and always in service to our primary purpose—presenting the voice of Dhūrjaṭi the man.

Hank Heifetz
Velcheru Narayana Rao

For the Lord of the Animals—
Poems from the Telugu

1

My chest has been worn away
by the breasts of women rubbing against it.
My skin has been roughened
with love scars from their nails.
Lost in the straining of passion, youth
has gone.
My hair has started falling out,
I'm sick of it all.
I can't go on in this circling world.
God of Kāḷahasti, make me
desireless.

2

In what form can my mind worship you?
Haven't men revered you as a kneecap,
a woman's breast, a measuring jar,
as a goat turd?
Heal my unease
and show me your real form so that
my eyes can be filled with you,
O God of Kāḷahasti, O drunken bee hovering
over the lotus of the mind!

3

So long as I am serving you,
let catastrophes come to me
or endless festivals,
let people call me
just an ordinary man or let them
praise me as a great saint,
let me be deluded by the pleasures of the world
or let Knowledge become mine,
let the movements of the planets
pull me down
or let sweet things happen!
Could any of it mark me,
O God of Kāḷahasti?

4

Because of your thinking,
"This man,
prey to great vices,
drunk with the liquor
of the pleasures of love,
has no awareness of me,"
you haven't cared to help
when I have been
drawn into the ocean of hell,
but if a boy who happened to be
lost in the pleasure of playing a game
should fall into a well,
then wouldn't
his father be concerned,
O God of Kāḷahasti?

5

Did I ever ask you to stand guard at my door
or be a whoremaster and bring me
heavenly dark-haired women?
Or have I given you food
soiled with my own spit while insisting
that you eat it up right away?
The only thing I ask of you
is that you save those well-meaning people
who trust entirely in you.
O God of Kāḷahasti, why,
O lord, why won't you hear me?

6

Those kings drunk with power,
serving them is like being in hell.
The things they give you—women with eyes
like lotuses, palanquins, horses, jewels—
all breed pain.
I've had enough of wanting them.
O God of Kāḷahasti, through your grace
change me so that I awaken
to the wealth that is Illumination.

7

Even though knowing that death
is near, still not willing to let go of life,
hoping for some physician to cure him,
some drug to save him, some god
who will have compassion for him,
the holy man who has performed his own funeral
while still alive, to break from the world, even he
does not think of you for an instant,
O God of Kāḷahasti!

8

Waves, trembling leaves,
glittering mirrors, lamps
in a wind, the flickering
ears of an elephant, vision after vision
of imaginary water, firefly light,
letters written on air, a single breath,
rice balls made of the milk of moonlight—
such is wealth.
Then why do men go blind with pride
about it,
O God of Kāḷahasti?

9

This is the contract between you and me.
Listen to it!
Without pay from you of even
one copper coin, I will serve you
always and with pleasure
in my mind
and you, do not give me over
to the band of enemies within me.
This is enough!
I don't want a horse,
I don't want an elephant,
and wealth is not what I want,
O God of Kāḷahasti!

10

There is no end nor any beginning
I can find for you
and you have never confided
your true image to me.
Why should I waste my time
in these worthless flutters of thought?
O God of Kāḷahasti,
I trust only in you whether you bathe me
in nothing but water
or whether you bathe me in milk.

11

What other devotees have done,
O God of Kāḷahasti,
I am unable to do.
I can't make my hands
throw stones at you.
I could not call out,
"My child, come run to me,"
then kill my son for you,
and I'm not someone who,
as an offering,
would tear out his eyes.
What is there to say for the way I am?
It's on your good will now
and my luck
that everything depends.

12

After they have been offered betel nut by a king,
or they have just heard themselves praised,
or their bellies are full of food,
or the Goddess of Wealth has given
        herself to them with all her graces,
or they have been listening to musicians
singing beautiful music—
those pretentious men who then become generous
to display their love
for the game of generosity,
is there anything worth saying about them,
O God of Kāḷahasti?

13

Did the spider study the Vedas
or the snake consult law books?
Did the elephant labor at spiritual disciplines
or the hunter intone a mantra?
Can learning be the source
of our awakening?
No! To worship your feet
with devotion,
O God of Kāḷahasti,
would be enough for everything
that lives!

14

Is that cave of pleasure filled with dirt
the doorway to *the suṣumna*?
And the hair around it, is that *kuṇḍalinī*?
Are feet, hands, and eyes *the six cakras*?
Is a face *the supreme cakra*
or a forehead *the crescent of the moon*?
Is making love *yoga*?
O God of Kāḷahasti,
why do men wear themselves out after women?

15

All of this is illusion, if you
think about it
and look!
but even when a man does understand,
he will always feel—
"women, sons, wealth, my body,
these are facts!"
and he wanders off
into the ocean of cravings.
Does he ever focus his thoughts
to the tiny extent of a tamarind leaf
on you who are supremely real,
O God of Kāḷahasti?

16

If a king is money-hungry,
how can there be any order?
How can there be any basis
for function and exchange among the many castes?
How can good people ever be happy?
How would the courtesans live by their beauty?
O God of Kāḷahasti,
how could your devotees worship
the lotuses of your feet?

17

If what you had was a craving for meat,
how could that have been any trouble,
when you hold a deer on the palm of a hand
with another arm raising a sharp sword
and fire alive inside your third eye
and the water of the Ganges in your hair
to be well cooked in the bowl of that skull you carry?
Was it fitting for you then, O God of Kāḷahasti,
when that tribesman
offered you meat he had soiled
with his own spit by tasting it,
for you to have accepted
and to have eaten?

18

Have I been disloyal to my lord?
Have I refused to listen
to your words?
Isn't it true that I look
nowhere else but to you?
I am innocent,
falsely accused.
Why do you submerge me
among the waves
of the ocean of sorrows,
keeping me there!
Is this justice,
O God of Kāḷahasti?

19

The mountain with its slopes of diamonds
resplendent with great wealth, where the
wish-granting cow
lives and the tree grows that gives everything,
is your bow.
The God of Riches is your friend.
The husband of the Goddess of Wealth
worships you fervently.
Is there anyone richer than you,
O God of Kāḷahasti?
You won't look at me! You aren't concerned.
Who will take away my poverty?

20

O God of Kāḷahasti,
your name
turns into fire
and destroys a mountain of faults
like so much cotton!
Should someone hear it,
even by chance
or at a distance,
he will escape injury
from the proud, uplifted arms of the God of Death
and will gain Freedom.
The shastras say this.
Great scholars say this.
How can anyone still have doubts?

21

I have lost the glory
of the lotus of my mind
because of the torrents of sins raining fiercely
down from the great lightning cloud
of life in the world.
The clear season of your compassion
when the storms have passed,
my god!
will be enough for me.
Through serving you,
with my mind in meditation,
I will flourish
like a blossoming field of lotuses!
O God of Kāḷahasti

22

The Moon is called King and there are stories
about his suffering,
and the god of riches, Kubera,
is called King and lost one of his eyes.
Suyodhana was called King
of the Hundred Kauravas and died
in battle along with all his kin.
The very word "King"
so sickens me,
I will never accept it
for myself ever, even
in some other life,
O God of Kāḷahasti.

23

Saying this is your wife, they bring a woman
and the knots are tied at the neck.
Then children come one after another
and the boys take their brides
and the girls are given in marriage.
O God of Kāḷahasti,
how did you fashion this worthless wheel
of family love that turns us,
cog meshing smoothly with cog around
and around?

24

The way in which I trust you,
I trust nobody else.
Other than you I have no one,
no older brothers, no younger brothers,
no mother, father, or guru,
none to help me when I am in danger.
My father!
Is there a day you will take me across
this mournful ocean of life
to let me float
in endless joy
on the ocean of milk,
O God of Kāḷahasti?

25

So long as I sleep under your roof,
O God of Kāḷahasti,
even the food a beggar gets
will do.
Were I to be granted inexhaustible riches, still
I would not serve these worms, these kings!
Don't bind me with ropes of hope
and move me around
for the sake of life with a family,
if you have kindly decided to accept me
as your servant

26

Haven't I taken your name
and sipped the water
that has washed your feet,
received the betel nut out of your mouth,
your platter
and your food offering,
and so become your son?
For anyone other than you,
I cannot bear to be a son!
It is right to accept me,
O God of Kāḷahasti,
to accept me and then never
again leave me

27

At doorway after doorway, the gatekeepers
smash their staffs down on the palms
joined in entreaty and add their curses
to the burning pain, but yet men eager
to serve the kings plead
even more to be let in,
among whom, craving
for the kingdom of the Goddess of Wealth,
go none of your servants,
O God of Kāḷahasti!

28

Fools complain that no sons
have been born to them
and they lose their way in desire
to live on after death.
Weren't uncountable sons born
to the King of the Kauravas?
What higher heaven did he gain
through having them?
And that holy man Śuka,
without sons did he suffer any hells?
O God of Kāḷahasti,
can the state of being Free
rot away if you have no sons?

29

Bad conjunctions of planets
and evil omens,
how can they trouble those best of men
who recite your blessed name
day after day?
Can a swarm of locusts
quench fire?
O God of Kāḷahasti,
it is beyond me
why human beings don't end their sorrows
serving you!

30

My mind is sickened but yet not quite.
It rejects
its delight in the youthful thighs of women
but yet
not quite.
It cuts down
the vine of desire that is the illusion
of riches, friends, sons
but yet not quite.
It offers its service
to you with love but yet
not quite.
O God of Kāḷahasti,
subdue its restless strength!

31

From those who follow other gods,
I will ask nothing,
not even with a will to save my life!
If I have something to ask,
I will go where they live
who revere the lotuses of your feet.
Since I have found you to worship,
what good is there in others
and what is there to ask?
Your grace is enough for me,
O God of Kāḷahasti!

32

Rutting elephants and carrying-chairs
and horses and precious jewels,
palanquins and women of the palace,
bright clothes and perfumes,
can they give Freedom?
Ah! Foolish men wishing for them
have wasted their days
waiting at the gateways of kings!
O God of Kāḷahasti

33

How long will I live?
What will I experience?
In the time to come,
whom will I protect?
With what form of concentration,
will I serve you?
When will ultimate joy,
without equal,
come to me?
How long from now will it be?
And should I remain as I am,
what will happen to me?
Do not make me feel small!
watch over me,
O God of Kāḷahasti

34

If every day in my mind
I can see you
sitting like a lotus,
blissful, on a stone pedestal,
in the mango grove by the shore
of the river Suvarṇamukhari,
that! that is the highest joy!
Can the enticing Goddess of Wealth
with her dance of illusions offer
any happiness at all?
O God of Kāḷahasti!

35

Make my body everlasting,
or if not,
find a way so that I may never
be born again after I die.
If you can't do either
of these two things, then tell me
at once that you're not able
and I'll do whatever I can do,
O God of Kāḷahasti,
to serve you and to find you
in the course of time

36

One protector of the earth
ruled for fourteen aeons.
The commands of another
throughout his long life
were obeyed for all the distance
from the Mountain of the East
to that of the West.
Hasn't the majesty of such kings
been revealed
to these insignificant people
full of aggression?
Why in hell do they clamor
and shout "We are kings!"
O God of Kāḷahasti?

37

If you call a man a king, must he then
say good-by to compassion,
charity, self-respect,
the tolerance that learning can give,
good-by to speaking the truth
and to helping scholars who have been his friends,
to gentleness or recognizing
whatever others have done for him
and good-by to loyalty?
O God of Kāḷahasti,
is there a reason why kings seem to be
a growth from the worst seed?

38

Those fortunate beings
whom once you anointed as kings
of the realm of Freedom
and I are alike!
Yes! You ask how?
Like them—the spider,
the young cobra,
and the elephant in rut,
my thoughts are filled with fierce violence!
The only difference
is that I have not found you
in my mind,
O God of Kāḷahasti!

39

Snakes as your ornaments,
the skin of a great elephant and
living as a hunter
have been things you loved
and so your releasing the snake
and the elephant and the hunter
from the sorrows of life
can be understood.
But that you honored a spider,
that you made it one with yourself,
and that you enjoyed
doing it!
Would you be kind enough
to let me know your reasons,
O God of Kāḷahasti!

40

Even if I were to sleep
with the women of heaven,
desire would not weaken
in the slightest.
Even if I were to gain
the power of the Creator,
I could not satisfy
my greed.
Even if I were to swallow every one of the worlds,
my wild, deep-seated rage
would not cease.
In these, there are no pleasures
that I desire.
O God of Kāḷahasti,
through service to you I will cross over
the great ocean of my faults.

41

Unless he throws off pride about wealth
and defeats the enemies within him,
burns down his desires,
slices away his weaknesses,
tears out the flaws that arise
from the sufferings of rebirth,
unless he cuts short the pleasures of youth
and slaps all lower divinities
across the face in contempt,
how can he possibly
see you, O God
of Kāḷahasti!

42

When mourners cry out over the dead
burning on the river bank, they will say,
"O God of Death! We are coming,
we as well, you can be sure of us,
we know it!" Then they take the cleansing bath
and the fools move on and they forget
the real weight of what they have said.
O God of Kāḷahasti

43

If I should pray to those worms who are kings,
would the suffering of living
go away as it only can
through worshiping your feet?
Can the pain of a child's hunger be soothed
by sucking at the dewlap of a goat,
O God of Kāḷahasti, instead of the breast
of the mother who gives him her milk
with love in her eyes?

44

A sword can turn into a flower,
and fire into cool rain,
and the ocean can be as stable as earth,
an enemy the best of friends,
and poison can become the food of the gods
for the man who never grows tired of saying "Shiva."
Shiva! Your name,
O Shiva! O God of Kāḷahasti!
is the source of every power.

45

Aren't there roots and fruit in the woods?
Aren't there caves? Isn't there water in the streams?
Aren't there beds of leaves?
Aren't you always there, in the soul,
with your pity,
to save those who are tired of the world?
O God of Kāḷahasti,
why do people go and serve kings?

46

I do not know how many times I have been born
before this birth, how many heaps
of sinful actions I have performed
out of ignorance. How many can they be?
Even if I try to think it out,
I cannot count them.
I want this one to be my final birth!
Please make it the last.
Show me your compassion,
O God of Kāḷahasti,
for what merit I have gained through serving you.

47

However long this body remains on earth,
for that long, watch over me
with your merciful gaze
so that terrible diseases may not flare up
to cause me suffering,
but afterwards,
O God of Kāḷahasti,
let me live,
meditating on the lotuses of your feet,
with a mind that will have abandoned
all the world of matter!

48

The water is the mood of emotion.
My flowers are arrangements of words.
My music is the resonance of lovely sounds.
The fine clothes are the figures of speech.
The lights are the radiance of the verses.
My offerings is the sweet flowing of the poem.
And so I worship you
in the way I know how,
O God of Kāḷahasti,
performing a magnificent service
bright with devotion

49

How can you be praised in elaborate language,
similes, conceits, overtones, secondary meanings,
or textures of sound? They cannot contain
your form. Enough of them!
More than enough. Can poetry hold out
before the face of truth?
Ah, but we poets,
O God of Kāḷahasti,
why don't we feel any shame?

50

If parents say to a child,
"Come and eat now, my son,
my precious son, get up now, quickly,
we'll give you rice and milk,"
and the child answers, "I won't eat
if you don't go and buy me some bananas,"
won't the mother and father then
soothe their child by bringing him the fruit
just like that
and, speaking a wealth of loving tender words,
O God of Kāḷahasti,
won't they feed him?

51

When you who ride the King of Bulls
are assaulted by the god of love
grown fierce,
it is your bull who turns
swiftly against Kāma,
he who carries you confronting
that untamed bull,
and when they angrily face each other,
I am in the middle,
like a calf ablaze with misery
crying out to you
to save me
as you have done before,
O God of Kāḷahasti!

52

What they call bad dreams,
omens, conjunctions of planets,
readings of palms, what they call
diseases caused by magic
or the evil eye, malevolent spirits,
all the varieties of poison,
how many traps
have you made for living beings
and still given them love
for their lives which cannot last longer
than the blink of an eye,
O God of Kāḷahasti!

53

He who places your offering of flowers on his head,
your ashes on his forehead,
your garland around his neck,
and the fragrance of your sandal paste
on the tip of his nose, he who swallows
your food offering, that devotee,
whoever he may be,
is your companion always,
roaming in pleasure on your silver mountain,
O God of Kāḷahasti!

54

Who am I to praise you
whom even the Vedas cannot comprehend?
I have begun, in prose and verse,
to describe your divinity.
Help me, make use of me
to write the sacred story of your existence!
Be my right hand.
Save my life! O God
of Kāḷahasti!

55

When men are kings
who are fools, whom anyone at all
can approach—no matter what sufferings
they may impose upon me
at any time, I shall not leave
the lotuses of your feet!
Whatever you may give me,
O God of Kāḷahasti,
will make me ruler
over the silver mountain of Shiva,
float like Vishnu on the ocean of milk,
or like Brahma sit with pleasure
at ease on the lotus.

56

So that your white mountain,
your garland of bones, your bull,
your skull, your tiger skin, your ashes,
and your ornaments of snakes would not be shared
with sisters, you resolved from the first
to be born without relatives.
Putting these kinds of troubles
at a great distance
was well and carefully done,
O God of Kāḷahasti

57

When those who worship you
and say that you
are the way
gain Freedom,
why do other people continually busy themselves
at their work for a living?
Haven't they heard the Vedas
crying out loud and clear,
"There is food for the span of your life!"
People take the wrong paths
stained by the darkness of this world
and so they do not see you,
O God of Kāḷahasti

58

"We have learned the Vedas by heart
and examined the greatest sacred texts.
We have developed the schools of philosophy
and, as a result, we have discovered,
'the body cannot last
and Brahman is truth,' "
they say, useless words
in the assemblies!
but of the unchanging joy that comes
from conquering one's own mind
they know nothing,
O God of Kāḷahasti!

59

Everything is unsure.
Everything in the daily process
of the body is sorrow.
Everything within
is a long line of pain.
Everything in the body
is confused, fearful.
Everything is
an endless stuffing of the body.
Being a man of flesh and blood
is a miserable way to live
and so in their meditation,
while they try to think of you,
people cannot reach you,
O God of Kāḷahasti!

60

While they make a show of being people
who have sworn they would
never write hymns of praise,
if they think of caring for their wives and children,
they decide the filthy kings
are worthy and go off to serve them.
O God of Kāḷahasti, how is this right?
I can't imagine myself singing
any man's life.

61

Why is it some people think of killing other
people and taking over their thrones?
Won't they die themselves, won't their wealth
leave them? Will they live eternally
with their wives and their friends and their sons?
Isn't death, O God of Kāḷahasti,
O isn't it coming
some day?

62

I never think of asking you to give me things,
so if you don't care for my poetry
I'll bear that all right.
It's only my tongue's natural work,
nothing other than my worship.
O God of Kāḷahasti,
how could I ever find you
if all I wanted of you
were my wishes?

63

When parrots see the bright red kiṃśuka flowers
and hungrily rush to them,
thinking them bunches of fruit, then
they are bitterly disappointed.
Learned men study the shastras
that are the roots of all grammar,
of every art and ritual,
and isn't that far and away
the wrong direction
to find what is eternal in the mind,
O God of Kāḷahasti

64

He who feels your compassion never enters the temples
of lower gods,
never speaks any begging words of prayer,
follows no one and pretends nothing,
serves no other belief in the world,
and no matter what trouble and pain he is put to,
does not suffer in this life,
O God of Kāḷahasti.

65

How do men live for so many years,
meditating on the depths of your nature,
at peace on the hills and in the forests,
without injuring anyone
or stealing anyone's money
or making love to other men's wives,
O God of Kāḷahasti?

66

Whenever people worship you,
requesting your grace,
isn't it true you give them
as much as they themselves have earned
by their observances?
As with food, there will be as much bread
as there was dough!
Why should anyone
receive the ease he wishes for without
worshiping you through right action,
O God of Kāḷahasti!

67

We all take pleasure in seeing
and smelling and hearing and tasting
and the touch of skin pressing against skin.
Why have you made us with these senses
if our using them is a sin?
What do you gain, O God of Kāḷahasti,
by playing this game of illusions
for your own amusement
to while away the time?

68

My relatives are traitors,
full of jealousy and hypocrisy and
always ready to do me harm.
I swear on my father's head
that they are beyond enduring,
but if I were to fight back even a little,
people would say I was wrong.
If only I could give up the world, go away,
be a sannyāsi and be free of *them*!
But I can't be free of the bitterness in my mind.
O God of Kāḷahasti,
where can I go?

69

Damn learned men ramble on
with the words they've studied
for playing all the games they can,
but when I step out, I lose my way
in a frightening jungle of doubt
where lust and anger stalk me like tribesmen
and fiercely attack, so that my mind reels.
Please hear what I say, O God
of Kāḷahasti.

70

Was it because once I stood
at your very threshold
which even Brahma cannot cross
and there tried, through shrewd planning,
to seize the wealth of Freedom,
that I am deprived of the daily
pleasure of worshiping you
and must suffer through hard times?
Is that why you now force me to cross
the thresholds of evil
king after king,
O God of Kāḷahasti?

71

It's a simple thing to be a guru
and graciously say to your disciples, "Here, take
this water I have used to bathe
my lotus-like feet. Your money,
your body, your life all
belong to me, your guru,"
but to be contemptuous of wealth
and through the way of non-action,
O God of Kāḷahasti,
to make you
                    rise up in the mind,
that is a difficult thing even
for a learned man.

72

Have they ground to dust
all the uncountable universes
born of illusion?
Have they been able to kill
the God of Love
whom no martial power
can conquer?
Have they had the strength to avoid
infatuation
with the deceiving Goddess of Wealth?
Have they effortlessly
conquered Death
which is the snake that ends life?
O God of Kāḷahasti,
how can any
of these other
gods offer us the Highest Good?

73

When I think of the past,
the terrible sinful
things I have done,
I am sickened by them.
When I see before me
that grim death after death
will come to me sooner or later,
I am frightened.
When I look at myself,
when I think of my actions,
terror descends upon me and
darkness falls across time.
O God of Kāḷahasti

74

I know I shouldn't curse Brahma
but why did he create learned men?
Well, if he did it because of his own great mind,
why did that slave give them hunger?
And if hunger had to exist,
O God of Kāḷahasti!
why did he fashion evil men
and make them kings?

75

When your devotees serve you
in a thousand ways and appeal to you,
why are you a miser?
Why don't you satisfy their desires
with compassion?
O God of Kāḷahasti,
think of their condition!
If you should grant them the Highest Good,
would that diminish
your holy treasury?

76

What is it that sickens you?
What does being sickened mean
when man's whole mind is sick?
What do you smear on yourself?
What does the smearing mean
since this whole body
is smeared with pride?
What is it that you clothe?
What does clothing mean
when you are always clothed in ignorance?
What is it that you do?
What does doing something mean?
None of it means anything,
O God of Kāḷahasti

77

I have attended to spells
and magic rituals.
I have been instructed
in the secrets of Sankhya and Yoga.
I have recited the Vedas and the shastras.
But my doubts have not been answered
even as much as a mustard seed
set down next to a pumpkin.
Give me faith,
O God of Kāḷahasti,
show me the way
to firm, stable knowledge.

78

Does it give me even a little ease
or make the wishes in my mind come true?
Can even the slightest crumb of it go along
with me when I die?
Will it bring me fame all over the world
or remove any of my faults?
Can it show you to me when
I need you, O God
of Kāḷahasti! Why can't you make
my craving for this circling world
just seep away?

79

If half a day passes,
with a little less food than usual,
it cannot endure it.
It looks for shade because
it can't bear the sun.
Afraid of the cold,
it tries to make a fire.
Whenever it rains,
it dashes into one house
and then another.
This body!
and how sad it is,
O God of Kāḷahasti,
that people do not get disgusted
with the pleasures it gives,
don't hope for its end!

80

Why do people go to Kedāra
or all the other
sacred places,
when by thinking of your feet,
won't a front yard become Benares
and a doorstep the mountain of Kailāsa?
O God of Kāḷahasti,
aren't people who make these pilgrimages
destitute
of the wealth of Knowledge?

81

When will you catch hold of my mind,
the thief that shows great energy
at glutting itself with stealing
women from other men,
money from other men,
and tie it with the ropes of renunciation
to the pillars of your feet
where it will be happy,
O God of Kāḷahasti?

82

The awareness of wealth
is its soil,
the passion for life
the water which feeds it.
Aggression is the opening bud
and lies are the leaves.
Terrible acts are the flowers
and its fruit are those faults
born of lust.
This is the bitter tree
that rises out of the mind,
O God of Kāḷahasti

83

Those who ask me to create poetry for you,
O God of Kāḷahasti,
and those who want me to write my poems down
for them to have
and those who with complete devotion
sing your sacred texts —
people like these are my real family,
but those of the same flesh
I sit on, how are they
related to me at all?

84

Haven't they seen people dying
yesterday, the day before,
and always?
If human beings, when they are troubled,
could find you,
then you would be their support,
but they can't stop
going off
after money.
How can they ever find you,
O God of Kāḷahasti?
Perhaps they'll never worship you
if you are not willing to protect them
though they offend you

85

He gave you food soiled by his tasting it
in the cup of a folded leaf.
He bathed you
with a jet of water out of his mouth.
He put his foot wearing its sandal
on your head.
And yet you made Kannappa
worthy of all this great honor with which
he glows!
O God of Kāḷahasti,
we cannot understand
the majesty in which you move

86

What kind of elegance
is your blanket of an elephant's hide?
Is that deadly poison a meal?
Is the skull of Brahma
a bowl to hold in your hand?
Is the ferocious cobra a garland for your neck?
Well,
if this is how you are,
O God of Kāḷahasti,
and he knew it, how
could the divine Nārāyaṇa
take your feet
like lotuses into his heart?

87

At the time when everything was water
while you took the form of a banyan leaf,
Vishnu thought he would rest on you
and feel himself at ease,
and there he grew
like a blossoming field of lotuses
without effort as he lay
on this tiny leaf,
because you were the cause of it all,
O God of Kāḷahasti!

88

O God of Kāḷahasti,
you who wear only the air,
your name is the latch that locks
the panels of the doorway of time,
your name is the hawk that attacks
the amazing snake that is the fierce tongue
flickering from the face like an anthill
of Citragupta who delights in miraculously
keeping account of our sins, your name
is the imperishable thunderbolt
that breaks the teeth of death!

89

If those kings who are thorns
for the world were even to offer me
ten thousand pleasures,
my mind would disdain them,
but show me a king
who is just and truthful
and compassionate, and I will regard him
as I regard you,
O God of Kāḷahasti,
and feel happy at the end of every day

90

Long ago, didn't you
give your devotees Freedom,
but why not today?
Well, people claim that
as someone grows older and older,
he becomes obsessed with himself,
he clings to what he may have.
It seems that's true!
O God of Kāḷahasti,
why won't you look kindly
on a good man
who every day
worships you in his mind,
ah! crying out for you to help him!

91

I have fallen into bad company
and I have done things that were wrong
in the back streets.
But if you were to say,
"I can't bear you anymore
nor will I accept you.
Go away!"
and you were to throw me out of your house,
I would hang onto the eaves.
Don't I have
a thousand things I want of you!
O God of Kāḷahasti

92

On the inside of a stone,
can there be clear water
carrying a splendor of lotuses?
Where the untouchables live,
do you find a brahmin family?
Why do you keep pretending
that it isn't so!
O God of Kāḷahasti,
why do you
push me away
because of my bad qualities?
Think through every beauty
of your own nature and then
show me your grace.

93

In a matter of hours, maybe two,
maybe three, maybe not, then
today or tomorrow,
at the end of the year
or some day,
just when we don't know,
these bodies of ours
will fall to earth,
and yet people
do not follow the path
of the right order of things,
O God of Kāḷahasti,
where they would come to feel
our love for your feet.

94

Are the finest elephants and horses
such rare things in this world?
Or rows of palanquins, or courtesans
moving sensually, or beautiful clothes,
many jewels, sons, and everything
else that satisfies desire?
O God of Kāḷahasti,
do they seem so wonderful
for a man who worships those feet
of yours that outshine the lotuses?

95

No more than a handful of water
or a single flower
for your hair,
offered with stable devotion
on this earth by a human being
can in the end bring him
the holy Ganges, the crescent moon
and you,
O God of Kāḷahasti,
for isn't your glory
all this vast world?

96

If men would look deep into the light
behind their own eyes
and there find their real selves,
they could gain that unity which is
the highest pleasure.
But what do we hear instead?
"Without a fault, glowing like lotuses,
they have the grace of lightning in movement!
Like the arrows of the God of Love,
they win their victories!" praising
women's eyes that are like
the eyes of deer,
O God of Kāḷahasti

97

They say
"The world is like the cloth
that vanishes if you undo the threads,
like a rope that is mistaken for a snake,
like a shell that flashes giving the illusion of silver,
like a pot formed only for a time
from clay,
like marble glowing red as it reflects
a hibiscus flower."
O God of Kāḷahasti!
All these intellectuals,
who cannot savor the bliss of awareness,
learning to put their trust in words,
the fools! fall back in a flash
to the world of cravings.

98

Dakṣa insulted you
and didn't you kill him?
Even Brahma had to suffer
discipline from you,
and yet there are these people you permit
to flourish, evil men who speak out to insult
the worshipers of your lotus feet.
You must have broken yourself off
from those who love you, or else,
O God of Kāḷahasti, how could you be quiet?

99

Don't you still have the trident
in your hand that destroyed the Elephant Demon?
Have the flames in your third eye died down
that burnt the God of Love to ashes?
How is it that you don't kill
your slanderers?
O God of Kāḷahasti,
have they done you some great good turn?

100

The battle, the fortress,
diplomacy and robbery,
doctoring, serving the kings,
trading in ships on the ocean
and powerful spells—
if they work for someone,
then the fruit will be very great.
But if control is lost
and the wrong things happen,
all that wealth will disappear
and the man's life will hang in the balance,
O God of Kāḷahasti.

101

Those who father a son or—
of equal merit—give charity,
build a temple,
pay for the marriage of a brahmin,
deservedly receive the dedication of a fine poem,
dig out a reservoir for the flow of water
or make a forest grow,
even such people
who've lived well
cannot go to the world
earned by those who have served you,
O God of Kāḷahasti.

102

"Great king!
There is a skillful poet here to see you.
He has a fine style, a natural gift,
and he benefits
those for whom he writes.
He never uses poetry
to attack."
"He has seen us once—
tell him to go away"
will be the answer
they give, these damn kings!
O God of Kāḷahasti

103

I have made a vow to offer
my poetry to none but you.
I have labeled myself your poet,
and tying a string around my wrist
I keep it there as a sign,
but this vow has no worth
that the world values.
How vile,
the way things are,
everything all
wrong,
O God of Kāḷahasti

104

O God of Kāḷahasti,
instead of serving you
so he might sit and hold court
on the royal throne of a liberated mind,
he spends his time with evil men,
torturing his own conscience,
serving kings too low to be touched.
And when they get angry with him,
the learned man
shows pain.
It's as if he were on fire
and trying to put it out
by pouring oil all over his body.

105

In town after town,
men who sing ordinary songs
now call themselves poets.
They go into places and explain their
                    songs to somebody
they happen to find
and they say to them,
"You are aesthetes! You know poetry!"
O God of Kāḷahasti,
substance and emptiness are not distinguished.
Poetry has been cheapened.
Where is it
good poets can go?

106

Before the teeth fall out
while the body still has its strength,
before women feel disgust,
before old age takes over
and inside the body
funny things happen,
before the hair goes white,
O God of Kāḷahasti,
then a man should contemplate
the lotuses of your feet!

107

Those who smear ashes
on their bodies
already covered with dust,
whose heads
are heavy with matted hair,
who have worn themselves out
enduring the pains of tapas,
on whose tongues
the five syllables of your mantra
live, O God of Kāḷahasti,
those who have thrown off the world
and are endlessly happy,
whose ornaments are rudrākṣa beads
and the glowing precious stones
of truth as it is being spoken,
I honor them,
whoever they are,
to whatever caste they were born.

108

I have had my satisfaction
with pleasures at the doorway of the King of Love
and those that have come to me through entering
the palace gates of many kings.
Now I want quiet. Show me
the doorway to the highest tṛuth
where, through your kindness,
O God of Kāḷahasti,
I can be at ease and at rest.

Notes to the Poems

Poem 2. The objects mentioned here all resemble the Shiva lingam in form. "A woman's breast" refers to a legend about two friends, one of whom, on the night of Mahāśivarātri, decides to spend the night sleepless at a temple of Shiva, as prescribed for Shaivites, while his friend visits a prostitute. The formally observant man, however, fills his mind with thoughts of the pleasure he is missing while his friend thinks of Shiva and regrets that he is not in the temple. At midnight, the man in bed with the woman worships the prostitute's breast as a substitute for the lingam. Since he has given up sleep and meditated on Shiva, the god emerges from the breast and gives him Liberation. The Shiva of this legend, known as *Ācaṇṭeśvara*, "The Lord of the Breast," has a temple dedicated to him at a village called Ācaṇṭa in Andhra Pradesh. According to another version of this story—narrated by Nori Narasimha Śāstri in *Dhūrjaṭi* (Madras: Trivent Publishers, 1971), a novel based on legends of Dhūrjaṭi's life—the man who worshiped the prostitute's breast was Dhūrjaṭi himself. Similar legends state that someone who worshiped his own knee, considering it as a lingam, found Shiva, as did another man who worshiped a goat turd. See Pālkuriki Somanatha, *Basavapurāṇamu* (2d ed.; Madras: Andhra Granthamāla, 1952).

Poem 7. A sannyāsi, or "renouncer," ritually performs his own funeral, *jivacchrāddha*, indicating that he is dead to this world.

Poem 10. The final statement, *nīran mumpumu pāla mumpumu*, stems from a Telugu proverb, *nīṭa muñcinā sare, pāla muñcinā sare*, literally: "whether [you] immerse [me] in water or [you] immerse [me] in milk"—meaning, no matter whether bad or good fortune comes.

Poem 11. A devotee named Siriyāla, according to a legend in the *Basavapurāṇa*, killed his son, cooked the body, and offered it as food to Shiva, when requested to do so by the god. For the story of Kannappa, who tore out his eyes, see the Introduction; for the story of Sāṅkhya Toṇḍa, who threw stones at Shiva, see Basavapurāṇa, chap. 6.

Poem 12. Betel (*tāmbūla*), consisting of betel nut and other ingredients wrapped in a leaf, was given along with gifts as a mark of honor. Literary descriptions indicate that patrons gave *tāmbūla* and gifts of new clothes to poets when works were commissioned.

Poem 13. For the legends of the spider, the elephant, the snake, and the hunter Kannappa see the Introduction.

Poem 14. The italicized words are technical terms of yoga. The terms relate to the so-called yogic body intuited by yogis in meditation and occur in texts describing sexual as well as nonsexual yoga. The *suṣumna* is a central channel in this yogic map of the body. *Kuṇḍalini* is a force, personified as female, which is said to lie coiled at the base of the spine. It is the goal of various yogic practices to arouse this force and make it rise along the *suṣumna* to the top of the skull, passing through the various *cakras* or "centers."

Poem 17. The descriptive details form part of the conventional iconography of the god Shiva. The legend of the hunter Kannappa is given in the Introduction.

Poem 19. According to mythology, Mount Meru, tallest of mountains, served Shiva as a bow when he destroyed the Three Cities of the Asuras with a single arrow. The God of Riches is Kubera. The Goddess of Wealth is Lakṣmi, whose husband is Vishnu.

Poem 20. Sacred texts, including the Vedas, are frequently called shastras.

Poem 21. Though the order of the poems in manuscript varies, this poem is always given as the first of the sequence. It shows the usual characteristics of such a first poem, which was normally composed after the rest of the *śataka* had been completed—elaborate Sanskritic imagery and a certain tone of having been produced to order rather than out of immediate emotional need.

Poem 22. In Sanskrit, *rāja* means "king" and also "moon." The Moon slept with Tāra, his teacher's wife, for which Bṛhaspati, the teacher, cursed him, causing him to wane. Kubera, the god of riches is also known as Rāja, and so was the prince of the Kauravas, Suyodhana (Duryodhana), king of kings, the adversary of the Pāṇḍavas in the *Mahābhārata*, where he is defeated in battle and loses his kingdom, his kinsmen, and his life. Kubera was struck blind in one eye because he happened to witness the lovemaking of Shiva and Pārvati. (See also the note on Poem 28.)

Poem 23. In a Hindu marriage ritual, the bridegroom ties a marriage thread around the bride's neck, making three knots.

Poem 24. "The ocean of milk," according to Puranic legend, exists during the immensely long intervals between the destruction and creation of universes. From it the gods and Asuras (Titans or anti-gods) working together churned *amṛta*, the Drink of Immortality.

Poem 26. The actions described at the beginning of this poem assimilate various ritual acts of devotion to behavior specifically characteristic of relations between a father and a son. A devotee, for example, may take the name of his god (as Dhūrjaṭi did) to identify himself as a sectarian, just as a son takes a family name. To eat from another's plate is an act of extreme intimacy in India, only sanctioned between immediate family members, while the devotee eats the food (*prasāda*) which has been offered on plates to the god, then blessed and distributed.

Poem 28. Dhṛtarāṣṭra, the patriarch of the Kaurava clan in the *Mahābhārata*, had a hundred sons, all of whom died in the battle of Kuruksetra, leaving no one to perform the annual rituals for him after his death. The sage Suka, the son of Vyāsa, never married.

Poem 31. The feet are the ritually lowest part of the body (which is why it is a great insult in India to strike someone with a sandal). To revere or bow down to the feet is therefore an act of complete submission or devotion. Calling the feet of the god "lotuses" emphasizes their beauty and purity.

Poem 38. The three beings of course were "anointed as kings of the realm of Freedom" through being taken into Shiva's heaven.

Poem 39. "The skin of a great elephant" is that of the Elephant Demon, Gajāsura, whom Shiva killed in battle. In the *Mahābhārata*, Shiva appears to Arjuna in the guise of a mountain hunter. The animals and the hunter mentioned in the latter part of the poem are those of the Kāḷahasti foundation legends.

Poem 49. "Similes" (*upama*), "conceits" (*utprekṣa*), "overtones" (*dhvani*), "secondary meanings" (*vyaṅgya*), "textures of sound" (*śabdālaṅkāra*)—these are all well-known terms of Sanskrit poetics, accepted in court poetry.

Poem 51. The King of Bulls is Shiva's mount, Nandi. The god of love, Kāma, is compared to the uncastrated bull (*ābotu*) who services the herds and who, in Andhra villages, is regarded with respect and often allowed to wander free.

Poem 53. Ritual items are consecrated by being offered to the god, thus becoming "his," even though they may then be worn or tasted by human beings.

Poem 55. The names Shiva, Vishnu, and Brahma have been added in the English translation.

Poem 56. The items mentioned here are Mount Kailāsa, where Shiva lives; Nandi, his bull; and various details of his iconographic appearance. These constitute Shiva's property. In a Hindu family, a man is expected to share his property with his sisters and give gifts to them at the time of his marriage.

Poem 57. "There is food for the span of your life"

(*āyurannamprayacchati*) is an often quoted Sanskrit aphorism.

Poem 70. This poem probably refers to Dhūrjaṭi's earlier practice of tantric rituals.

Poem 71. The word translated as "guru" is *ayyavāru*, a term for Vaishnavite gurus. This is an implicit sectarian thrust by the Shaivite Dhūrjaṭi.

Poem 72. The four events referred to here are Shiva's periodic destruction of the universe, his burning Kāma—the god of love—to ashes (when Kāma attempted to fire a flower arrow at him), his ascetic's vow of poverty, and probably the story of the sage Markaṇḍeya, who clasped the Shiva lingam at the point of death whereupon Shiva appeared and stayed the hand of the death god, Yama.

Poem 74. The word "slave" (*gulāmu*) is used here as a term of general abuse against the creator god, Brahma.

Poem 85. The story of Kannappa is given in the Introduction. The events described here violate a whole series of brahminical taboos. The food, a hunter's meal of meat and toddy, is in itself unclean as an offering for Shiva. Furthermore, it has been tasted by the hunter and, except in the case of immediate family, food is polluted by the touch of the saliva of another person. The foot is the ritually lowest part of the body and to put a foot on a head indicates extreme insult. Kannappa in the legend places his foot on the eye of the lingam (and therefore symbolically on Shiva's head) in order to prevent the eye of the lingam from watering while he is tearing out his own.

Poem 86. For the "elephant's hide" see the note to

Poem 39. The poison is the *Hālāhalam* poison which rose from the ocean of milk and was swallowed by Shiva in order to protect the world. (It turned his throat blue-black.) Brahma once had five heads, one of which was cut off by Shiva who wears it as an ornament in his hair. Nārāyaṇa is a name of the god Vishnu and so the statement is a sectarian assertion of the preeminence of Shiva.

Poem 87. Here a Vaishnavite creation legend is slanted toward the worship of Shiva, since the poem stresses the temporal and essential superiority of Shiva.

Poem 88. Citragupta is the accountant of Yama, the god of death. He keeps records of people's sins and reports to Yama when punishments are to be assigned after death. In India, snakes frequently live in large anthills.

Poem 97. These are similes used by the philosophers of Vedanta to illustrate the illusionary status of the physical world.

Poem 98. Dakṣa was the father of Shiva's first wife, Sati. He insulted his daughter and her husband by failing to invite them to a sacrifice and then ignoring his daughter when she nevertheless arrived alone. Sati then committed suicide (later to be reincarnated as Shiva's second wife, Pārvati). As a result of this insult to Shiva, Dakṣa was destroyed. For the reference to Brahma see the note to Poem 86.

Poem 101. The actions referred to in this poem are known as the *sapta santāna*—"the seven kinds of progeny" or "Seven Sons"—and are considered to be of equal merit.

Poem 102. "Poetry to attack"—*ṭiṭṭu kavitvam*,

"curse verses," were used by poets to curse patrons who did not give them gifts. If, for instance, certain syllables occurred in certain places in a line, the verse was believed to have a power which would destroy the person to whom it was addressed.

Poem 103. "But this vow has no worth / that the world values"—*lokul mecca vratambu nā tanuva kīlun nerpulungāvu.* The original reading is corrupt. This is the best interpretation we can make of it.

Poem 105. "Men who sing ordinary songs"—*bavinini gāḷḷu*, a type of folk singers who sing praise-songs for śūdra castes.

Poem 107. "Tapas," conventionally and stiffly translated as "austerities," is a word derived from the Sanskrit root *tap*, originally meaning "to heat," then "to generate magic heat or power through ascetic practices," and, by derivation, "to suffer pain"—or, more loosely, to perform any sort of ascetic practice, including purely mental acts of concentration. The concrete magical sense of the word (it is often used colloquially in modern Indian languages) is not readily translatable and the Sanskrit word has therefore been retained as a collective, singular noun. The mantra is *nāmaḥ śivāya*, "Homage to Shiva." Rudrāksa beads are handsome brown seeds with furrowed surfaces worn as necklaces by devotees of Shiva.

Poem 108. "Doorway of the King of Love" is a metaphor for the vagina.

Afterword

Telugu literature is conventionally divided into two streams, the Sanskritic tradition called *mārga* and the indigenous tradition called *deśi*. *Mārga* ("mainstream") literature developed under the patronage of kings, while *deśi* ("local") literature originated outside the courts and later in the medieval period found support in the temples. Dhūrjaṭi lived and wrote during the Vijayanagar period, which is usually regarded as the golden age of Telugu literature. The work of Dhūrjaṭi shows influence from both traditions. In this Afterword a brief outline is presented of the background of Telugu literature, intended to provide an overview of the context, both historical and ideological, of Dhūrjaṭi's poetry.

The formal history of court poetry in Telugu commences with King Rājarājanarendra (reigned 1018–1062) of the Cāḷukya dynasty. A Telugu version of the *Mahābhārata*, begun by Nannayya, his court poet, is the earliest extant work of Telugu literature. A rich tradition of court poetry continued, with important variations in style and content, until almost the end of the seventeenth century. During the long history of *mārga* poetry, spanning almost six hundred years, a continuing relationship develops between the king and the poet. This relationship undergoes complex changes which are also reflected in the nature of the works produced. An overview of this long tradition yields a broad division of the patron-poet relationship into three major modes. The modes of poetry, too, follow the same pattern.

The Poet and the King as Guru and Disciple

King Rājarājanarendra and the poet Nannayya provide a classic example of the first mode of relationship between the poet and his king, that of guru and disciple. In his preface to the Telugu *Mahābhārata*, Nannayya describes the setting in which his royal patron commissioned him to compose the *Mahābhārata* in Telugu.[1] He depicts the king seated in splendor among his court, surrounded by ministers, generals, attendants, grammarians, scholars of various disciplines, poets, musicians, and courtesans. The poet Nannayya is also there and gives a long description of himself in the words of the king. He is the king's family priest and well-wisher; he is pure, has performed many rituals, is learned in sacred texts and

1. The passage describing Rājarājanarendra's court summarizes Nannayya's *Śrīmadāndhra Mahābhāratamu*, 1.8–20.

traditional narratives. He is a great storyteller. He never lies and in intellect he is equal to the teacher of the gods. Then the king informs Nannayya that he himself has listened to all the sacred narratives, learned the codes of law, enjoyed great poetry and drama, and venerated the most revered scriptures, but he still prefers, above all, to listen to the *Mahābhārata*. He cares most about five things: pleasing brahmins, listening to the *Mahābhārata*, worshiping the god Shiva, giving charity, and associating with peaceful people. The *Mahābhārata* is also the story of the king's ancestors, the Pāṇḍavas, who were born from the Moon. Consequently the king requests Nannayya to retell the Sanskrit *Mahābhārata* of the great Vyāsa in Telugu, and the poet modestly accepts the task.

This description illustrates the mode of relationship between the king and the poet where the poet is seen as the guru and the king as his disciple. The patron's aspirations are meant to reflect his desire for spiritual advancement and religious merit (in this case with a strong Jain emphasis).[2] The poet on the other hand, is depicted as possessing the purity and wisdom required to help the king attain his aspirations. The desire of the king for a prestigious connection with the legendary heroes of sacred history is linked with

2. The Jain influence on Nannayya's description of his king has received little attention. The epithets used by Nannayya for his king, unlike those used by later poets, do not glorify war, and Nannayya describes his king as a peaceful man, *śāntuḍu*. Even the valor of the king is presented in metaphors of peace and self-control.

these moral motives. It is the poet who can legitimize and publicize this connection.

During the period when this mode of relationship prevailed, the poets composed narratives retold from the ancient Sanskrit *itihāsas* and *purāṇas*.[3] Tikkanna continued the Telugu version of the *Mahābhārata* begun by Nannayya. He was a poet at the court of Manumasiddhi, a twelfth-century king of Nellore. Though his continuation of the *Mahābhārata* was dedicated to the god Hariharanātha (a composite form of Vishnu and Shiva) and was not commissioned by his royal patron, another work of Tikkannna, the *Nirvacanottararāmāyaṇa*, a poem on the later story of Rāma, was commissioned by and dedicated to the king. Ĕrrāpragaḍa, the third poet who had a hand in the completion of the Telugu *Mahābhārata*,[4] was a court poet of Prolaya Vemārĕḍḍi, a fourteenth-century king of Addaṅki, and composed the Telugu *Harivaṃśa*, the Vaishnavite appendix to the *Mahābhārata*, at the request of his patron.

The patron-poet context described by Nannayya

3. The genres of *itihāsa* and *purāṇa* include the *Mahābhārata* and the *Rāmāyaṇa* (which are *itihāsas*) and the major *purāṇas*, eighteen in number, many of which were retold in Telugu during this period. Though the terms are used somewhat loosely, *itihāsa* may be translated as "heroic narrative" and *purāṇa* as "myths and religious legends."

4. Though Nannayya began the Telugu version of the *Mahābhārata*, he completed only two and a half of the eighteen books of this epic. Tikanna began with the fourth book and composed all the remaining fifteen books. Ĕrrāpragaḍa composed the half of the third book left unfinished by Nannayya, as well as the *Harivaṃśa*, thus completing the work. The three poets are called *kavitrayamu*, the poet-trio.

established a paradigm for many centuries to come. When the poet Śrīnātha, in the fifteenth century, was commissioned, by a brahmin minister named Māmiḍi Siṅganna, to compose a Telugu version of Śrīharṣa's Sanskrit *Naiṣadhīyacarita*, the details of the context followed the same mode as was set by Nannayya, three centuries earlier. The patron is made to praise the poet Śrīnātha as "one who has gained the knowledge of supreme reality as described in the sacred texts."[5] The text commissioned here, however, was not a sacred text, like the *Mahābhārata* or the *Rāmāyaṇa* or the *purāṇas*. It was an erotic poem, based on the story of the love of Nala and Damayanti, borrowed from the *Mahābhārata* and reworked by Śrīharṣa in Sanskrit. Nevertheless, the poet retains the role of the holy and learned person who is credited with knowledge of the great religious texts and therefore is superior to the patron. In this case, the patron was not even a king but a minister aspiring to kingly status. The poet provides that status through describing his patron with symbols appropriate to a king.

The Poet and the King as Friends

By the time of the Vijayanagar empire, and especially the reign of Krishnadevarāya (1509–1524), the rela-

5. The phrase is a summary of the quotation:
brahmāṇḍādimahāpurāṇacayatātparyārthanirdhārita
brahmajñānakaḷānidhānamavu.

Śrīnātha, *Śṛṅgāranaiṣadhamu*, 1.13.

tionship between the king and poet changes into one of friendship and companionship. The conventional descriptions of this period follow the paradigm set by Nannayya, except for the fact that the poet is no longer a guru superior to his king. The patron does not seek spiritual advancement from the poet, nor does the poet have the status to dispense it. Instead, the patron seeks fame and entertainment from a poet whom he treats as his friend. Here is how the court poet Allasāni Pĕddanna describes the royal court of Krishnadevarāya in his preface to the *Manucaritramu*, the story of the birth of Manu:

Women with faces like the autumn moon, their eyes shining out
like dark lotuses, were waving chowries
and scholars were discussing the details of the sutras
of Kaṇāda, Pāṇini, and Bādarāyaṇa
while guards stood nearby, fearless men with terrifying
swords of blinding brightness,
and tributary kings surrounded him with the soft light
radiating from their brilliant gems
as the glittering rays from the jewels on his war anklet
that marked him as "Master of the Three Kings" were dancing
all around the borders of his white silk garment which
then seemed to be of many quivering colors.

While he sat in splendor in his assembly hall
called "Conquest of the Universe," discoursing with his scholars,
his heart was moved by the sweetness
of poetry and, from his throne, he spoke to me with kindness.

"Among the Seven Sons which bring one fame,
only the poem does not perish on this earth!
Therefore compose a poem for us, noble Pĕddana!
with words sweet as nectar and soft as the *śirīṣa* flower.

"You are my friend. You are the vessel of gracefully
elegant speech. You who know the meaning of the great
purāṇas
and *āgamas*, legends and stories! Father
of Telugu poetry! Who can be mentioned beside you?"[6]

With this poet, Allasāni Pĕddanna, a new genre called the *prabandha* acquired definitive form, in which narrative was reworked into an elaborately descriptive poem. A *prabandha* is defined by the number of descriptions it contains, generally listed as eighteen (an auspicious number) but almost always more. These are supposed to include descriptions of such subjects as a city, seasons, sunrise, moonrise, marriage, lovemaking, the birth of a son, hunting, battle, and so on. The focus of the *prabandha* is on the aesthetic quality of the descriptions and not on narrative or character development. The grandeur of the *prabandha* consists in the ornamental beauty of language, in luxurious description and intricate detail. It is a text to savor, to relish, and the notion of

6. Allasāni Pĕddanna, *Manucaritramu*, 1.12–15.
All the poems in this afterword have been translated in collaboration with Hank Heifetz.

sanctity acquired through listening to the story is far less important than in the case of *itihāsas* and *purāṇas*.[7]

The Poet as Servant of the God-King

During the period of the Nāyak kings in Tanjore (16th–17th centuries), the relationship between king and poet changes once again. The king comes to be regarded more as the god Vishnu than as a man representing an aspect of Vishnu. The role of the poet in the court of the god-king becomes that of a servant (*dāsa*) of the god. The court poet sings not only for the king but about the king. The preferred

7. *Prabandha* in Telugu incorporates the features of *sargabandha*, the poem divided into chapters, as defined by the poet and aesthetician Daṇḍin in the *Kāvyādarśa*, ed. with Telugu commentary by Pullela Sriramachandradu (Hyderabad: Andhra Pradesh Sahitya Akademi, 1981). Daṇḍin says (1.14–19):

sargabandho mahākāvyam ucyate tasya lakṣaṇam
āśīrnamaskriyāvastunirdeśo vāpi tanmukham

itihāsakathodbhūtam itaratra sadāśrayam
caturvargaphalāyattaṃ caturodāttanāyakam

nagarārṇavaśailartucandrārkodayavarṇanaiḥ
udyānasalilakrīḍāmadhupānaratotsavaiḥ

vipralambhair vivāhaiśca kumārodayavarṇanaiḥ
mantradyūtaprayāṇājināyakābhyudayair api

alaṅkṛtam asaṅkṣiptaṃ rasabhāvanirantaram
sargair anativistīrṇaiḥ śrāvyavṛttaiḥ susandhibhiḥ

sarvatra bhinnavṛttāntair upetaṃ lokarañjakam
kāvyaṃ kalpāntarasthāyi jāyate sadalaṅkṛtiḥ.

poetic form of this period is the *yakṣagāna*, a kind of musical drama, often composed by royal princes or by courtesans. The daily activities of the king and the love of his women for him are the major themes.[8]

The Vijayanagar Period

In the classical age of Telugu literature, the Vijayanagar period (1300–1600), poets enjoyed sustained patronage not only from the reigning kings but also from ministers, chiefs of armies, local rulers, flourishing merchants, and even village accountants. Poets were good image makers and also symbols of status. Being so important, they were also expensive, and the lives of such poets could be fairly comfortable, so long as their patronage lasted. Inscriptional evidence, which is extensively available, and descriptions by poets themselves indicate that poets who were able to enter circles of patronage lived in luxury. Often the land of entire villages was granted them, free of rent.

In return for gifts received, the poet addressed a poem to his patron and wrote a long series of verses describing the genealogy of the latter in idealized terms. This was one of the preferred means for a family to move up into one of the desired social

8. For a survey of poets and their works during this period see Niḍadavolu Veṅkaṭa Rao, *Dakṣiṇadeśīyāndhravāṅmayamu* (Madras: Madras University, 1978).

classes (*varṇas*). Many lower caste families, which were usually consigned to the low category of *śūdras*, aspired to be considered equivalent either to *kṣatriyas* or *vaiśyas*. In the operation of the very complicated social mechanism available to families, the poet was a significant factor. He provided the necessary status symbols by glorifying the family in verse. Public recitation of such verses by the poet apparently took place at a ceremony where the work was dedicated, which signified social recognition of the patron's status.

In the case of ruling kings, the poet did an additional service. Sovereignty as a concept recognized by Sanskritic Hinduism is a divine feature of Vishnu. The king was the representative of this divine aspect on earth. In his prefatory verses, the poet would recognize the superior status of the reigning monarch. This was accomplished by providing a fictitious origin for the royal patron from the Moon, which ensured inclusion of his family in the *kṣatriya* class. The other features which were necessary for sovereign status were (1) ability to control enemies, always being victorious in battle, and (2) youthfulness and physical charm, always being attractive to women. These two images were related; both were a sort of conquering. The land which the king ruled was spoken of as *bhūsati*, the "earth-wife." A king was considered the husband of the country he ruled. The people (*prajā*) were his progeny. The victorious battles he fought were often presented in images of sexual prowess, while his sexual attraction for women was described in terms of battle imagery. The two patterns reinforced each other.

Related to this was the literary presentation of polygamy. Just as the king has innumerable victories in battle, he has many wives and countless courtesans, an image that intensified his quality of sovereignty. The dedicatory poem to him was also referred to as a woman. Receiving the dedication of a book was metaphorically equivalent to marriage with the *kṛtikanya*, the "poem-virgin" or "bride that is the poem."

The opening and concluding verses of each chapter of a *kāvya* were utilized by poets to elaborate on the idealized personal qualities of the royal patron. The style used in these sections was more heavily Sanskritized than that in the body of the text. Sanskrit was the language of gods and ritual, the only language that could ensure legitimization of status. It was, of course, not well understood except by a small number of learned brahmins and other high caste persons, but its power as a vehicle of legitimization was supreme. In a paradoxical way, its unintelligibility and sacred status were connected. A language, to be ritually powerful, had to be beyond normal intelligibility.

For all apparent purposes, the poet was only describing his patron. In effect, however, he was creating his patron. The image he was casting of his patron was to be (under ideal circumstances) accepted by the community. That the poet was conscious of his key role in the process is indicated, for example, by the following poem included in a fourteenth-century anthology:

The ocean dried out
on the point of Rāma's arrow

like a dewdrop
at the tip of a blade of grass.
And Rāma killed the ten-headed demon.
These stories would be lies
if Vālmīki had not written the Rāmāyaṇa.
The world encircled by oceans
would not know
whether a king lifted Mount Meru itself,
if he did not have a poet
to write about him.[9]

In a similar way, the patron also "made" his poet. The recognition he gave to a poet by admitting him into his presence and agreeing to receive the dedication of his work legitimized the status of the poet. Great poets were those who lived in the courts of great kings. Great kings were those who had great poets in their courts. The equation was so perfect that a poet who was outside the royal court risked being a minor poet, and the poet without a patron was no poet at all. As a popular Sanskrit aphorism stated, "The bracelet shines because of the gem, and the gem shines because of the bracelet." The poet and the king shone because of each other.

Such an ideal situation of mutual dependence in image making is best illustrated by the legends about King Krishnadevarāya's court. A great poet is metaphorically described in literary convention as an elephant among poets. Symbolizing his conquest of the universe, Krishnadevarāya, the legend says, was served by eight great poets, representing the Eight Elephants of the Directions, the *aṣṭadiggajas*.

9. Madiki Siṅganna, *Sakalanītisammatamu* (Hyderabad: Andhra Pradesh Sahitya Akademi, 1970), p. 4.

He has gone down in legend as a monarch in the field of letters as well as on the battlefield. It has always been difficult to identify the eight poet-elephants historically,[10] but the power of the legend is so great that it has survived even the most skeptical chronological inquiries of modern times.

The prefaces of nearly every work of court poetry serve as documents of valuable historical information, giving not only facts such as names and places, but also indicating how the facts were utilized and perceived through literary conventions. The picture that strikingly emerges is one of perfect harmony and glory. Nearly every patron had great qualities and lived in glittering luxury, and nearly every poet was unparalleled for his excellence. Stylized expression molded under the pressure of literary conventions filtered out all conflict and led to an extended picture of absolute stability and balance. Such a picture was too glorious to be real.

The Temple Poets

While the court poets and their patrons were engaged in mutual image building and admiration, another group of poets reflected a contrasting situation. These were the poets who often were associated with temples and who took the temple deity as their patron. These poets, whom we might call temple poets, served the

10. K. A. Nilakantha Sastri, *History of South India* (Madras: Oxford University Press, 1955), p. 412.

deity of the temple in much the same way as the court poet served his king. The temple poet sang on almost every ritual occasion in the temple, dedicated his works to the temple deity, and received gifts from the temple endowment. The temple poet did not recognize the sovereignty of the human king.

It is customary to classify temples as based on a pan-Indian deity—Vishnu temples or Shiva temples or goddess temples. While this classification has its advantages, it masks an important aspect of Hindu temples—the personal identity of the deity. Nearly every temple in Andhra is the home of a particular deity with a name and a biography of his or her own. The temple in Tirupati is, for instance, the house of Veṅkateśvara, concerning whom there are specific legends of birth and marriage and relationships to other deities. Veṅkateśvara is also Vishnu, for those who look on the deity as a manifestation of one of the supreme gods. But for the devotee, he is a person with a specific name, just as King Krishnadevarāya is a different person from Aḷiya Rāmarāya or King Anapotā Rĕḍḍi from Kāṭaya Vemā Rĕḍḍi.

It is important to recognize the individuality of a temple deity when considering the relationship of the poet to his god. The temple poets looked upon their deities as their lords, whom they served, whose greatness they sang, and who, in their view, were the only power to whom they owed allegiance. Since their "kings" were gods, the king who sat in the palace was only a human being. The position of temple poets gave them the strength necessary to reject invitations from kings.

Legends about temple poets make opposition to

human power represented by kings a tradition which continued to influence literature even into the twentieth century. The first such opposition is reflected in the legends about Tāḷḷapāka Annamācārya (1424–1503), who made the temple at Tirupati his home and the deity Veṅkaṭeśvara his Lord.

Annamācārya sang only for his deity and composed thousands of songs for him. According to legend, Sāḷuva Narasiṃha Rāya, a king of Vijayanagar who ruled from 1487 to 1490, commanded him to sing songs like the ones he had composed for Lord Veṅkaṭeśvara. Annamācārya refused, saying that he recognized no Lord other than Veṅkaṭeśvara. King Narasiṃha Rāya chained the poet-singer and threw him into prison. Annamācārya sang for the god and his chains miraculously fell away. The king then realized his error and prayed for forgiveness.[11] A similar story is told about the poet Potanna (15th century), a resident of Ekaśilānagaram, the modern Warrangal in the Telangana area of Andhra Pradesh. Potanna dedicated his *Bhāgavatamu* to his personal deity, Rāma, and stated in his work that the god appeared in a dream and commanded him to "speak" the *Bhāgavatamu* in Telugu. There is a legend which says that he rejected a request from a local ruler for the dedication of the *Bhāgavatamu* to himself. The king was angry and had Potanna's manuscript buried underground. As a result, parts of the palm-leaf manuscript were eaten by termites. The destroyed

11. Tāḷḷapāka Cinnanna, *Annamācāryacaritramu*, ed. Vēṭūri Prabhākara Śāstri (Tirupati: Tirumal Tirupati Devasthanams Press, 1949), pp. 37–40. The author was the grandson of Annamācārya.

sections were restored by Potanna's disciples. Many manuscripts of the *Bhāgavatamu* include a verse approving of Potanna's dedication of his work to the god Rāma rather than to the king. The verse, considered by some editors as an interpolation, is as follows:

Rather than giving his poems to lowly kings
and receiving money and mounts and dwellings,
then aging and dying and suffering
the hammer blows of the God of Death,
this man, Bammĕra Potarāju, has, of his own will,
uttered his poem to be given to Śrī Hari
for the sake of the welfare of the world.[12]

Yet another legend about Potanna relates that while he composed his *Bhāgavatamu*, the goddess of poetry, Sarasvati, appeared before him with tears in her eyes, fearing that he might, like all the other poets, sell her to the kings. A verse in oral circulation describes how Potanna reassured her:

Beloved daughter-in-law of Vishnu! Wife of Brahma!
O my mother! Why do you weep so that the tears
fall to your breasts from your eyes dark with collyrium?
I will not, out of hunger, sell you, neither in thought
nor word nor action, to these meager kings of Karnataka
who are nothing but merchants. Trust me, Sarasvati![13]

12. Bammĕra Potanna, *Śrīmadāndhramahābhāgavatamu*, 1.1.11 (Hyderabad: Andhra Pradesh Sahitya Akademi, 1964).

13. Cāgaṇṭi Śeṣayya, *Āndhrakavitaraṅgini* (Kapileshvarapuram, Andhra Pradesh: Hindu Dharma Sastra Grantha Nilayamu, vol. 6, 1961), p. 180.

While the temple poets rejected royal patronage, the kings themselves adopted devotional relationships to the deities of major temples. Prominent among such kings was Krishnadevarāya, who visited many important temples as a devotee and gave them generous grants of land. He prominently publicized these visits, which established his devotion to the deity and thus his position as a ruler under the protection of the god. Krishnadevarāya even had images of himself and his wives in attitudes of devotion cast in bronze and set up in the main hall of the temple at Tirupati.[14]

Krishnadevarāya's court poet Allasāni Pĕddanna takes care to state in his preface to his *Manucaritramu*, that the king was only the bearer of the burden of the earth, similar to *ādiśeṣa*, the primeval snake; *ādivarāha*, the primeval boar; *kūrma*, the tortoise; or the *aṣṭadiggajas*, the Eight Elephants of the Directions. The king was not Vishnu; he was only sharing an aspect of Vishnu in ruling the earth under the prescriptions of the ancient laws given by Manu. Describing King Timma, an ancestor of Krishnadevarāya, Pĕddanna says,

Timma, become mighty, greatest of the lords of the earth,
relieved the illusionary tortoise and the mountains,
the king of snakes, the Elephants of Space,
and the ancient boar of their burdens, for he
carried the earth on the pedestal of his arms,
where it was secure, and the brilliance of his fame
spread through the air between earth and sky and,

14. Krishnadevarāya, who was himself a poet, dedicated his *Āmuktamālyada* to the god Veṅkaṭeśvara of Tirupati.

as his enemies at either side of him humbly
served him, he displayed his raging power.[15]

This was the Sanskritic/brahminic conception of the role of the king. Yet at the same time as this position was stated by Pĕddanna, another court poet of Krishnadevarāya, Nandi Timmanna, who wrote the *Pārijātāpaharaṇamu*, presented a very different image of the role of the king:

Because as a cowherd he could not sit on a throne,
he was to take his place, radiant, on a throne.
Because he made love to the wives of other cowherds,
he was to act as a brother toward all women not his own.
Because he lost Mathurā to the demon Jarāsandha,
he was to take by force the fortresses of his enemies.
Because he had greedily stolen Indra's Pārijāta tree,
he was to wipe out that blemish with his charity.
Because all these faults had to be his when born
before as Krishna, he has returned so as to remove them.
He is Krishna descended again, who has taken on a form
that receives utmost honor from everyone in the world:
the son of Narasarāya, Krishnarāya, lord of the earth.[16]

For Timmanna, the king Krishnadevarāya was the god Krishna himself. Identification of the god in the temple with the king in the palace was customary in the south, where indigenous traditions were still dominant. To Timmanna, who came from the south-

15. Allasāni Pĕddanna, *Manucaritramu* (Madras: R. Venkateswar and Co., 1919), 1.23.
16. Nandi Timmanna, *Pārijātāpaharaṇamu* (Madras: Vāviḷḷa Ramasvāmi Śāstrulu & Sons, 1968), 1.17.

ern tradition of poetry, service to the king and service to the deity in the temple were not contradictory. It was this style which became more prominent later during the period of the Nāyak kings, who ruled from Tanjore, a city in the southern Tamil country.

But in the medieval Andhra region, which combined the strands of Sanskritic and local ideologies of kingship, the Sanskritic ideology was dominantly expressed in the court poetry. This helped to sharpen the differences between king and god and heighten the contrast between the temple poets and the court poets.

Though the court poets attempted to present a glorious picture of every patron who sponsored their work, the political atmosphere was not as stable as it is made to appear in their polished verses. Political upstarts rose to prominence by ruthless elimination of contenders to the throne, even their own elder brothers, fathers, or uncles. Petty local landlords attempted to gain the glory of major kings by manipulating the resources of power and the symbols necessary to establish it. Except in the case of a powerful ruler like Krishnadevarāya, the court poet did not always have stable and sustained support.

The image of the temple poet evidenced from legends was one of simplicity and voluntary poverty. Our poet Dhūrjaṭi speaks repeatedly of the palanquins, elephants, and fine clothes which the court poets acquired from the kings. Although some temple poets like Tyāgarāja (1767–1847) did live in poverty, not all were poor. In the insecurity and changing fortunes of royal dynasties in medieval Andhra, the temples were relatively stable and some of them were very wealthy. One such temple was that at Tirupati, the home of the poet Annamācārya. He, his wife, and his sons and grandsons were all poets who not only lived a comfortable life in undisturbed literary and devotional pursuits, but made expensive gifts to the deity of the temple.[17] In contrast, Śrīnātha, a poet who served many kings during the fifteenth century, is recorded as having fallen into bad days when the Vijayanagar dynasty was overrun by the Gajapatis of Orissa. Deprived of his patrons, Śrīnātha was too poor even to pay the rent on his land and was punished for his failure to obey the law. Similarly, Pĕddanna laments the death of Krishnadevarāya and regrets that his life after the death of his patron was worse than death.[18]

Nevertheless, the popular image of the temple poet as a poor and noble person who entrusted himself to his god and of the court poet as a seeker after riches given by kings continued to dominate literary folklore. The stereotype of the court poet is represented by Śrīnātha, who, according to legend, visited Potanna as the latter was ploughing his farm. Śrīnātha attempted to persuade Potanna to dedicate his *Bhāgavatamu*

17. Tāḷḷapāka Annamācārya composed, according to the literary evidence, some 32,000 songs about Lord Veṅkaṭeśvara of Tirupati. These songs were preserved on copper plates. The Oriental Institute in Tirupati has 2,701 copper plates on which are inscribed the literary works of the members of the Tāḷḷapāka family. Among these, Annamācārya's works amount to 2,284 plates. For details see Vĕṭūri Ānanda Mūrti, *Tāḷḷapākakavula Padakavitalu: Bhāṣāprayogaviśeṣālu* (Hyderabad, 1976).

18. Verses circulating in the oral tradition, attributed to Śrīnātha and Pĕddanna, describe their situations.

to the king. Potanna, according to a verse circulated orally, replied:

Instead of giving the virgin poem, tender as the fresh buds
of a young mango tree, to evil men, rather than eat
food earned through trade in women, what does it matter
if good poets become peasants, what does it matter if they
dig up roots in the depths of the forest so that they may
feed themselves and their wives and their children?[19]

In court poetry, metaphors are used of the poem as a virgin and the royal patron as her husband. The temple poetry of Potanna here subverts the metaphor. The poet who composes his poems for the king is equated with the pimp who trades in women.

The court poet, in his role as the companion of the king, mirrored the status of the king. The titles of the court poet indicated his position as king among poets. Śrīnātha was known as Kavisārvabhauma, the "emperor of poets." Just as the king did not tolerate anyone equal to him in his realm, the court poet competed with and defeated, in scholarly dispute, any poet who claimed superiority among poets. Śrīnātha had a famous contest with the poet Ḍiṇḍima, court poet of Vijayanagar. Ḍiṇḍima, who also was known as "emperor of poets," exhibited a bronze drum as a symbol of his high position in the realm of letters. Śrīnātha challenged his claim, defeated him in open contest, and, in a dramatic demonstration of

19. Attributed to Potanna, this verse circulates in the oral tradition. Niḍadavolu Veṅkaṭa Rao records this verse as well as the legend around it in his *Potanna* (Delhi: National Book Trust, 1962), p. 128.

his victory over Ḍiṇḍima, had the bronze drum broken in public court.

The symbols of status held by the court poet reflected the symbols of the king. He had the right to be carried on a palanquin, have an umbrella held above his head, and wear pearl necklaces and gold-embroidered clothes. The honoring of a court poet included *gajārohaṇa* (seating him on an elephant), and *kanakābhiṣeka* (pouring gold coins over his head).

As the companion of the king, the court poet reflected the status of the king. He was, in a sense, the king's alter ego. The king is presented as always attractive to women, but his sexuality is somewhat problematic. As David Shulman points out, the South Indian king is surrounded by "ambiguous rings of women who define the varied frustrations of his love—cold and barren courtesans, passionate but remote admirers, faceless queens."[20] His romantic life is never happy and he is never to be infatuated with a woman. The court poet, on the other hand, is represented as always pursuing women and is not depicted as attracting them by his mere presence. In the vigor of his sexuality, he is similar to the king, but he has the liberty, not permitted a king, to pursue women actively.

The court poet was a *rasika*, interested in all the pleasures of the senses. A well-known poem attributed to Pĕddanna speaks of the comforts and pleasures required to compose poetry:

20. David Shulman, *The King and the Clown in South Indian Myth and Poetry* (Princeton, N.J.: Princeton University Press, 1985), p. 339.

Without a quiet place, without a betel nut flavored
with camphor sent by my lover through her
dear friend as messenger, without a good meal
that I find delicious, and a swinging cot,
and men of sensibility who can tell what
is good from what is bad, and the best of
scribes and performers who will understand the intent
of my work—unless I have all of these—
can anyone possibly ask me to compose poetry?[21]

The temple poet, in contrast, has the image of a saint. He is opposed to luxuries and never seeks sexual pleasures. Biographical legends about temple poets typically depict them as uninterested in the pleasures of the world since early childhood. In the ideology of temple poetry, the court poet's interest in pleasures and the eroticism of his poems are equated with immorality and obscenity. The court poet's image of a *rasika* is subverted to mark him as a libertine, a person of no moral character.

This saintly image of the temple poet is all the more interesting, given the prominence of eroticism in temple poetry and its frequent detailed explicitness. In court poetry, however, the theme is human sexuality, while for the temple poet the participants are the deities of the temple, resulting in an eroticism removed from the realm of human beings. Both types are usually classified as *śṛṅgāra* (the Erotic), but when the deities of the temple are the subject, the encounters acquire—for those with a devotional perception—a

21. Verse from the oral tradition, quoted in Śiṣṭā Lakṣmīkānta Śāstri, *Vijayanagarāndhra Kavulu* (Vijayavada: Nirmalā Publishers), p. 296.

quality distanced from human sexuality. Eroticism of this kind includes the very same themes and descriptions employed by the court poets but context makes the difference.[22]

In addition to his role as a companion of the king, the court poet was also his attendant, forming part of a group that included the courtesans, the drummers, and the musicians. The services of the attendants to the king possessed a ceremonial status recognized as a feature of the monarch's sovereignty. According to the ideology of the temple, however, there is only one monarch—the deity in the temple. The human king in the palace only shares an aspect of the divinity. In the presence of the god, he is one with other human devotees. A radical position in this temple ideology is represented by poets who accept no royal status and no claims to sovereignty by any human power. From this position, the courtesans of the human king are seen as only whores and the court poet, by extension of metaphor, as a "male whore." Literary folklore reflects this position in several tales attributed to the legendary court jester and poet Tĕnāli Rāmaliṅgaḍu (about whom a number of stories are available from the oral tradition). Allasāni Pĕddanna, one story goes, was sitting on his swing cot wearing the *gaṇḍa-*

22. Traditional Telugu literary scholars discourage study of the eighth canto of Kālidāsa's *Kumārasaṃbhava*, because it describes the lovemaking of Śiva and Pārvati, who are the father and mother of the universe. The poeticians of the court tradition insist that a description of the lovemaking of parents is repulsive. The same kind of description, however, is perfectly acceptable in the temple tradition. Annamācārya and Kṣetrayya have many songs describing the lovemaking of the god and his consort.

pěṇḍeramu, the victory anklet, newly awarded by King Krishnadevarāya in recognition of the poet's superior status among all his peers, when Tĕnāli Rāmaliṅgaḍu visited him. Pĕddanna said proudly, referring to his anklet:

What does the golden anklet say that never stops jingling
on the left foot of the poet of Andhra and its voice is like
a lofty peacock? You! Tell me what does it say?

Now the king had a concubine, Gudiyala Sāni, to whom he gave lavish gifts as rewards for her skill. Tĕnāli Rāmaliṅgaḍu answers Pĕddanna in verse that precisely parodies the tone of the question:

It says in a hundred ways, that the line of fortune
which crosses the soft mons of Gudiyala the whore
isn't there for you on your forehead, it's not there!

In keeping with the aristocratic tradition of militant boastfulness, the court poets also described themselves proudly, claiming high levels of excellence in poetic skill and in scholarship. Some made more pompous claims than others, but all aspired to be considered the finest of their time. The only poets accepted as superior were the great ones of the past—again like the king, who admitted the superiority only of legendary ancient monarchs.

In contrast, the temple poet did not speak much of himself. He was the servant of a god and claimed no scholarship, no skill, and no superiority. It was through the god's grace that he was composing poetry. The god was the real speaker and the poet was only the voice through which the divine words were expressed. Rarely did the temple poet make claims of superiority over other poets or claim the right to elaborate titles.

The oppositions between temple poetry and court poetry were not limited to the popular images of the court and the temple. There was also a contrast in the poetics and aesthetics of these two styles of poetry. Court poetry, like life in the court, was heavily controlled by elaborate conventions. Dhūrjaṭi himself, in his *Kāḷahastīśvara Māhātmyamu*, relates the following illustrative legend.

A poor brahmin devotee of Shiva had nothing to eat since his crops had failed due to a severe drought. Shiva pitied him and gave him a poem, which he composed about the ruling king of Madurai. The king was a great patron of literature and would give a thousand gold coins to anyone who composed poetry and received the praise of the connoisseurs of his court. The brahmin took the poem, which was composed in the *śṛṅgāra rasa* (Erotic Mood), and presented it in the royal assembly. A poet in the assembly, Natkīra, objected to a description in the poem which said that women's hair by nature has a pleasant fragrance. His objection was that such a description was against poetic convention. The poor brahmin, who was totally ignorant of poetry, returned to Shiva, embarrassed, and gave the poem back to him. Shiva then himself appeared in the assembly to defend his verse, protesting that Natkīra was jealous. He asked the members of the assembly to show him what was wrong with his poem. Was it the *lakṣaṇa* (features) that were at fault, the *alaṅkāra* (embellishment), or the *rasa* (sentiment)? Natkīra repeated his earlier objection, to which Shiva responded by saying that Pārvati's hair had a naturally pleasant smell. Natkīra replied that what was true of a goddess did not apply to humans. Shiva was angry at him and showed his fiery third eye. Natkīra did not waver. "You may have eyes all around your head but your poem is still blemished," he replied. Shiva was furious and cursed Natkīra to become a leper.[23] The story, borrowed from Tamil tradition, is utilized by Dhūrjaṭi to focus on the conflict between court poetry and his own. Shiva's personal experience was valid for Shiva; Pārvati's hair, without perfumes, possessed a pleasant fragrance. For the court critic, however, personal experiences did not count. His concept of poetry was based on obedience to a set of poetic conventions, known as the *kavisamayas*, that had been handed down by tradition. Poetry could not be left to the personal vagaries of individual poets. It was regulated by the authority of the *alaṅkāra śāstra* (the Sankrit treatises on aesthetics), which prescribed how *devas* (gods) and *mānavas* (humans) should be described. The hierarchy could not be shifted. Verisimilitude was not the issue; it was a matter of observing laws. Precisely who had made the laws was never stated. The authorities were referred to as the ancients. If a name was ever mentioned, it was always that of a sage or a seer, divinely inspired and infallible. The critics in the establishment monitored observance of the laws and attacked deviance. In the literary tradi-

23. Dhūrjaṭi, *Kāḷahastīśvara Māhātmyamu* (Madras: Vāviḷḷa Rāmasvāmi Śāstrulu & Sons, 1966), 3: 131–222.

tion of medieval Andhra, even great poets like Kālidāsa did not escape censure. In a way, the model is analogous to the ideal social order where the divine Veda was the authority, while the brahmin *purohita* (family priest) was the interpreter, and his interpretations governed the king, who executed the law. *Kāvyajagat*, the world of poetry, though said to be independent and free from the real world, still had the same organization and hierarchy as the real world. Figure 1 indicates the homology between the two worlds.

The world of people

The world of poetry

Veda	Law	*alaṅkāra śāstra*
purohita	Interpreter	*ālaṅkārika*
King	Executor	Poet
People	Subjects	Cultivated readers

Figure 1. The homology between the ideal world of people and the ideal world of poetry

Natkīra, the court scholar, does not recognize personal experience as valid or necessary. He attacks even the supreme deity merely on the basis of scholarship. Shiva curses Natkīra to suffer from leprosy. Especially for one accustomed to the luxuries of court life, there could be no worse shock than to be suffering suddenly from a horrible disease. Later in the story, Natkīra is caught by a cannibal demon who shuts him into a cave, so that he can come back and consume him. These two experiences, the fear of losing his body to disease and the fear of losing his life, profoundly disturb the complacent scholar. He becomes a devotee of Shiva, ultimately is cured of his affliction, and achieves Shaivite liberation.

Poetry that comes out of agony and suffering can be understood only by people who know, or at least can have empathy with, such experiences. Dhūrjaṭi's *śatakamu* belongs to the category of poetry which courts did not appreciate. A poetry of pain and suffering, agony and distress, could not interest a court which was highly structured and controlled, and distanced from real life.

The Sanskritic tradition of court poetics stands in sharp contrast with Dhūrjaṭi's concept of poetic experience. *Rasa* in Sanskrit poetics is not an emotion. It is rather the *idea* of an emotion, depersonalized through the process of conventional observations. Distanced from life, with all personal passions filtered out of them, the *rasas* (emotional moods) represent a nonworldly, transcendent beauty, *alaukika saundarya*. It is important to recognize that the emotion of love which a person actually experiences, for example, is not *śṛṅgāra rasa*. It is just plain *kāma*, sexual passion. Similarly a person's grief is not *karuṇa rasa* (the Pathetic Mood). It is only grief. The aesthetics of court poetry are aesthetics of distance and ideation, rather than immediacy and feeling. The personal experiences of the poet, if there are any, are dissolved in the sea of faceless abstractions through meticulously controlled and ordered literary elements in strict adherence to accepted conventions.

Qualities like individual style and subjectivity,

The court poet was to select one of the ancient stories as his theme; any effort to create a story of his own was discouraged. Innovation was not considered a prerequisite to creativity. Using old materials and creatively rearranging them was regarded as the best approach to poetry. Excellence lay in varying, not in inventing.

In literary legend, Dhūrjaṭi is firmly included among the court poets. Literary critics of Andhra have long insisted that he belonged to Krishnadevarāya's court and that he was one of the *aṣṭa-diggajas*. Legends about his position in the court relate to his sensual style of living as well as his excellence at poetry. In keeping with the conventions of making the court poet a *rasika* (a sensual aesthete), legends about Dhūrjaṭi associate him with courtesans. Once, King Krishnadevarāya, who loved Dhūrjaṭi's skill in poetry, presented the first part of a poem to his court poets in the form of a puzzle:

Why have the words of Dhūrjaṭi, poet of Andhra, acclaimed talent,
taken on a sweet majesty beyond compare?

often identified by modern critics in court poets, were never pertinent to traditional criticism. There were no such things as individuality and individual style recognized by the *alaṅkāra śāstra*. On the contrary, the success of the court poet was based on his ability to approximate an impersonal model. Just like religious ritual, which was not created by any one individual but was to be followed by everyone according to prescription, the literary conventions too were to be followed and never questioned.

The poets were expected to answer the puzzle by completing the verse. Tĕnāli Rāmaliṅgaḍu completed the verse, according to legend, as follows:

Ah, I know!
It's because he quenches his thirst by continually drinking
the sweet honey flow from the lips of bold, graceful
courtesans.[24]

Dhūrjaṭi's work does show considerable evidence of a knowledge of royal courts and of courtesans. Not only does the *Kāḷahastīśvara Śatakamu* show his acquaintance with and passionate rejection of court life and its decadence, but his other work, the *Kāḷahastīśvara Māhātmyamu*, also shows him to be acquainted with the ways of courtesans. In a long story of two courtesans who rejected the prostitution which was their hereditary occupation in favor of devotion to the Lord of Kāḷahasti, Dhūrjaṭi elaborately describes the instructions their mother gives them on how to become successful at their trade.[25] Such information drawn from Dhūrjaṭi's works has led scholars to believe that, most probably, he did belong to one court or another for a time and that he rejected that position and became a poet associated with the temple at Kāḷahasti.

This does not, however, make him a temple poet like Annamācārya of Tirupati. A temple poet was

24. An oral verse frequently quoted. It can be found in the Introduction to Dhūrjaṭi's *Kāḷahastīśvara Śatakamu*, edited by Niḍadavolu Veṅkaṭa Rao (Hyderabad: Andhra Pradesh Sahitya Akademi), p. 89.

25. Dhūrjaṭi, *Kāḷahastīśvara Māhātmyamu*, 4:6–135.

ritually involved in serving his Lord, singing for him during all the services which took place in the temple. He was part of the establishment of the temple, which was modeled after a king's court. He was, in fact, the "court poet" of a divine "king." Dhūrjaṭi was not a temple poet in this sense. He might have left the king's court, but the court did not leave him. As his poems show, he was too passionately opposed to kings for him to disregard the court entirely and serve his divine Lord in peace.

The Genre of the *Śataka*

Telugu *śatakas* (this is the Sanskrit word, more properly *śatakamu* in Telugu) developed outside the courtly tradition. The earliest *śataka*-like text is probably the *Śivatattvasāramu* of Paṇḍitārādhya (13th century). This text has 489 poems addressed to Shiva. With Pālkuriki Somanātha (later in the same century), the *śataka* developed into a recognized genre. Amṛtānanda Yogi, a writer on poetics, defines a *śataka* in his Sanskrit work *Alaṅkāra Saṅgraha* as a text containing 108 poems.[26] This indicates a scholarly

26. *śatena śatakaṃ proktam aṣṭottaraśataṃ param*. Amṛtānanda Yogi, *Alaṅkāra Saṅgraha*, chap. 11, as quoted by K. Gopalakrishna Rao in his *Āndhra Śataka Sāhityamu* (Hyderabad, 1976). Other sources for a survey of *śataka* literature are Vanguri Subba Rao, *Śatakakavula Caritramu*, 2d ed. (1951); Vedam Venkata Krishna Sharma, *Śataka Vāṅmaya Sarvasvamu* (1951); and an excellent article (published as a small monograph), B. Aruṇa Kumari, *Śataka Sahiti* (Waltair: Andhra University Press, 1979).

recognition of the *śataka* as a literary genre. Taking into consideration the features of a large number of Telugu *śatakas*, the form may be described as follows: A *śataka* consists of a number of independent poems, usually more than a hundred. All are in the same (or slightly variant) meter and are addressed to a deity or a person. Each poem ends in a vocative called the *makuṭa* (literally, "the crown"), from which the *śataka* acquires its name. Thus Dhūrjaṭi's poems end in the vocative *śrī kāḷahastīśvarā* ("O Lord of Śrī Kāḷahasti"), and the collection is therefore called *Śrīkāḷahastīśvara Śatakamu*. While the auspicious number is stated as 108, the actual number of poems varies from *śataka* to *śataka*. Evidence suggest that poets composed each of the poems independently and, as the number grew larger, they would then be grouped into a *śataka*. The first poem of a *śataka* begins with the auspicious syllable *śrī*. Many *śatakas* also have a concluding poem recording the name of the author as well as other information, such as the date of composition. Other than the opening and concluding ones, the poems in a *śataka* stand on their own with no fixed connection to those preceding or following. There are also instances where a large number of poems of one or more authors, not intended as *śatakas*, were collected together and later called *śatakas*. Poems attributed to Vemana (*Vemana Śatakamu*) and those addressed to a fictitious "wise man" (*Sumatī Śatakamu*) belong to this category. As *śatakas* became popular in later Telugu literature, authors added features from court poetry such as the description of a patron who asks them to compose a *śataka*. The popularity of the *śatakas* is primarily due to their flexibility. A *śataka* does not have to restrict itself to a prescriptive code of grammar or poetics. As a genre originating outside the court tradition, *śatakas* also provided room for expression of the poet's opposition to such tradition. When the addressee of the *śataka* is a supreme deity, the poet is protected from the risk of insulting his human superiors. The freedom to speak to their god allowed the poets to speak their minds. Authors of *śatakas* did not aspire to literary recognition. No royal court ever recognized a *śataka* writer as a superior poet. Poets who excelled in standard court poetry and received the recognition of the scholarly establishment often composed *śatakas* as an act of personal devotion, but they never expected these works to be recognized as superior poetry. Such authors often used two different styles of composition—one for their courtly poetry and another for their *śataka* texts. Dhūrjaṭi, for example, conforms to the standards of prescriptive grammar and poetics in his *Kāḷahastīśvara Māhātmyamu*, but in his *śataka* he relaxes and uses spoken expressions and unconventional usages which would have been frowned upon in a courtly poem. The origin of the *śataka* outside the court had a formative influence on its development as a medium for personal expression.

Śatakas were almost always read by individuals for their own enjoyment. In this way they are different from texts like the *Mahābhārata* and the *Rāmāyaṇa*, which were performed for a group by a skilled reciter, and the courtly *kāvya* texts, which were read to an expert audience of scholars and critics. Since there was no silent reading in the Telugu tradition (silent reading came into use only after printed prose became popular), a poem from a *śataka* was always sung aloud within the private space of the individual, who was his own listener.

Early *śatakas* were primarily devotional, but gradually *śatakas* of many different kinds came to be produced: collections of moral instruction, philosophical exposition, humor, eroticism, or practical wisdom. As the *śataka* form became more and more popular, even humorous texts addressed to cats and dogs were composed. There were *śatakas* written for courtesans and mistresses. During the early twentieth century, *śatakas* were addressed to King George V and Mahatma Gandhi. Thousands of *śatakas* exist in Telugu, and no other genre has so many texts. Composed by poets from all stations of life, the *śataka* is the most accessible extended Telugu form, both for poets and for their readers.

Recent scholars of the *śatakas* have classified them under *bhakti* (devotional), *śṛṅgāra* (erotic), *nīti* (behavioral), *vedānta* (philosophical), *hāsya* (humorous), *cāritraka* (historical), *jīvacāritraka* (biographical), *svīyacarita* (autobiographical), *kathā* (narrative), *nighaṇṭu* (lexical), *jantu* (animal), and so on. These classifications are by no means definitive, since a number of *śatakas* include poems that belong to more than one classification.

If the contents of *śatakas* are not easily classifiable except for purposes of reference, like books classified in a library, it is even more difficult to talk about the stylistics and aesthetics of *śatakas*. The language of *śatakas* varies from a very dignified and elevated style to the common and homely, and even the obscene. A discussion of the aesthetics of the *śataka* therefore is not possible, but its poetics could be schematized. A poem in a *śataka* is a vocative statement; it is addressed to either a deity or a person. All literary texts are communications from a speaker to a listener, but the addressee of a *śataka* is not exactly the listener. Instead he is strategically placed as the neutral outsider positioned between the speaker and the listener so that when the text is read he merges either with the speaker or with the listener.

By the time Dhūrjaṭi was using the *śataka* genre, it had been well established in the *deśi* tradition, formed by the early Vīra Shaivite poets. They used the *śataka*, as may be seen in Pālkuriki Somanātha's *Vṛṣādhipa Śatakamu*,[27] and the *Sarveśvara Śatakamu*[28] of Yathāvākkula Annamayya (1232–1270), for an expression of ecstatic devotion to the deity and an exposition of theological concepts intended as a means of contemplation for the devotee. The *Nārāyaṇa Śatakamu*,[29] which is attributed to Bammĕra Potanna, is a series of poems addressed to and in praise of Vishnu. For Dhūrjaṭi, this devotional use of the *śataka* form is combined with a drive toward personal lyric and a tension, always present, between the man and his image of the divine.

Velcheru Narayana Rao

27. Pālkuriki Somanātha, *Vṛṣādhipa Śatakamu*, with commentary by Banḍāru Tammayya and Nūtikaṭṭu Koṭayya (Kākināḍa: Śri Nirmala Śaivasāhiti Granthamāla, 1969).

28. Yāthāvākkula Annamayya, *Sarveśvara Śatakamu*, ed. Kāśīnāthuni Nāgeśvara Rao (Madras: Āndhra Patrikā Press, 1925).

29. *Nārāyaṇa Śatakamu*, ed. Kāśināthuni Nāgeśvara Rao (Madras: Āndhra Patrikā Press, 1925).

A Note on Telugu Meter

Traditional Telugu meters are syllabic and quantitative. As previously mentioned, we have chosen to translate these poems according to meaning units, the way in which they are delivered in oral presentation. On the printed page, they are four-line stanzas. An identical quantitative pattern of short and long syllables, which varies according to the specific meter, must be followed in all four lines. As with classical Latin and Greek verse (and Sanskrit), short syllables are those that contain a short vowel, and long syllables those that contain a long vowel or a short vowel which is followed by two consonants.

Two other restrictions apply to the poetic line: *prāsa* and *yati*. *Prāsa* is the required alliterative identity of the second consonant in each line. *Yati* (which in Sanskrit signifies a caesura) indicates, in Telugu meter, the requirement that a specific syllable in the body of the line must chime (through an identical or related consonant and vowel) with the initial syllable of the line.

The poems of the *Kāḷahastīśvara Śatakamu* are composed in two different meters, both based on Sanskrit models. *Śārdūlamu* ("The Tiger") consists of nineteen syllables, with the *yati* at the thirteenth, and the following fixed pattern of shorts and longs:

L L L s s L s L s s s L L L s L L s L

The example which follows is poem 1 of our translation. The *prāsa* is marked with two underlinings and the *yati* chime with three.

kāyalgācĕ vadhūnakhāgramulace kāyambu vakṣojamul
rāyan rāpaḍe rommu manmathavihārakleśavibhrāntice
prāyambāyĕnu baṭṭakaṭṭĕ tala cĕppan rota samsāra me
ceyan jāla viraktu jeyagadave śrīkāḷahastīśvarā.

The other meter is *Mattebhamu* ("The Wild Elephant") and consists of twenty syllables with the *yati* at the fourteenth. The quantitative pattern is

s s L L s s L s L s s s L L L s L L s L.

This is poem 8 in our translation:

taragal pippalapatramul mĕruguṭaddambul maruddīpamul
karikarṇāntamu leṇḍamāvula tatul khadyotakīṭaprabhal
suravithīlikhitākṣarambu lasuvul jyotsnāpayaḥpiṇḍamul
siru land ela madāndhu lauduru janul śrīkāḷahastīśvarā.

A Note on the Text

Many editions of the *Kāḷahastīśvara Śatakamu* have been printed. There are also several manuscripts of the text in the Madras Oriental Manuscript Library. The printed editions slightly vary in the number of poems included. The variation is much greater in the case of manuscripts. The longest manuscript contains 129 poems, the briefest 21. Though no critical edition exists, most printed editions follow a fairly uniform, popular version of the text.

We primarily consulted the following editions:

Kāḷahastīśvara Śatakamu. Edited by Kāśināthuni Nāgeśwara Rao. Madras: Andhra Patrikā Mudrālayamu, 1926.

This edition contains 119 poems and incorporates textual variations from several manuscripts.

Kāḷahastīśvara Śatakamu. Edited by Niḍadavolu Veṅkaṭa Rao. Hyderabad: Andhra Pradesh Sahitya Akademi, 1966.

This edition contains 119 poems.

Kāḷahastīśvara Śatakamu. Edited by Bulusu Veṅkaṭeśvarlu. Kākināḍa: B.V. & Sons, 1962.

This edition contains 116 poems.

For our translation we chose 106 poems common to these three editions. When the text of a particular verse varied among the three editions, we followed the reading given in the Andhra Pradesh Sahitya Akademi edition.

In addition, we have chosen two poems from the edition published by Ārya M̃udraṇālayamu, Rajahmundry, Andhra Pradesh (poems 54 and 65 in the translation), which are not included in the three printed editions mentioned above.

Not only does the number of poems vary from text to text; the order in which they appear also varies, with the exception of the opening poem, which is common to all the printed editions as well as to the manuscripts. Because we rearranged the poems in this translation, we give here a list showing how the order of translated poems corresponds to the order of the poems in the Andhra Pradesh Sahitya Akademi edition.

Number of the Translated Poem	*Number of the Original Poem*
1	14
2	15
3	12
4	5
5	16

Number of the Translated Poem	*Number of the Original Poem*
6	18
7	34
8	23
9	4
10	19
11	17
12	11
13	13
14	49
15	3
16	22
17	20
18	6
19	7
20	10
21	1
22	21
23	36
24	24
25	25
26	26
27	91
28	28
29	29
30	32
31	30
32	31
33	33
34	35
35	37

Number of the Translated Poem	*Number of the Original Poem*
36	38
37	39
38	40
39	41
40	42
41	87
42	43
43	44
44	45
45	46
46	47
47	48
48	50
49	51
50	52
51	60
52	53
53	54
54	from Ārya Mudraṇālayamu edition
55	56
56	57
57	59
58	58
59	61
60	63
61	67
62	65
63	66
64	68
65	from Ārya Mudraṇālayamu edition

Number of the Translated Poem	*Number of the Original Poem*
66	93
67	75
68	69
69	70
70	2
71	3
72	74
73	76
74	83
75	95
76	71
77	77
78	79
79	80
80	81
81	82
82	85
83	86
84	89
85	118
86	90
87	119
88	97
89	98
90	96
91	101
92	102
93	104
94	105
95	106

Number of the Translated Poem	*Number of the Original Poem*
96	107
97	108
98	109
99	110
100	111
101	112
102	113
103	114
104	115
105	117
106	116
107	102
108	62

Transliteration of Telugu and Sanskrit

Only a few non-English words, almost all of them proper names, will be found in the translations; but the Introduction, Afterword, and the various bodies of notes contain a number of words and quotations from Telugu and Sanskrit. The following remarks are meant to provide approximate sound values for those unfamiliar with Indian languages. They do not offer a complete pronunciation guide to either language.

Telugu is a South-Indian Dravidian language, very different in phonetic structure and original vocabulary from Sanskrit, an Indo-European language closely related to Latin and classical Greek; but Telugu has assimilated a vast number of Sanskrit words, and classical writers especially made heavy use of these Sanskritic additions. We have used the standard, modern transliteration for Indian languages. In the case of three names (Vishnu, Shiva, and Krishna as in the name Krishnadevarāya), we have not used transliteration but have given them in the forms with which they have been received into English. All

Sanskritic words and names are spelled as they are in Telugu. (Feminine nouns and names ending in long *ī* or long *ā*, for instance, or the name of the god Brahma—which also requires a final long *ā* in Sanskrit—are given with their Telugu short endings.) When no specification is given, the following transliterations hold for both Telugu and Sanskrit words. Some important differences are noted separately.

Vowels and dipthongs are to be read as follows:

a like the *u* in but
ā like the *a* in father
i like the *i* in pill
ī like the *i* in machine
u like the *u* in put
ū like the *u* in rule

ṛ is a short vocalic *r* as in some Slavic languages. In the Telugu pronunciation of Sanskrit, it is normally read as *ru*, with the *r* trilled.

e in Sanskrit is pronounced like the *ay* in p*ay* but as a single continuous sound, not diphthongized. In Telugu there are two *e* sounds. Long *e* is pronounced like the Sanskrit *e*. Short *ĕ* is rather like the *e* in English b*e*t but slightly prolonged. All Telugu words given in transliteration have the short *ĕ* marked as such.

ai like the *ai* in *ai*sle
au like the *ow* in *now*

o like the *o* in n*o*. The same remarks made above for *e* hold for *o*. Short *ŏ* in Telugu is rather like *aw* in English r*aw* but somewhat prolonged. Telugu words will have the short *ŏ* marked as such.

All these vowels (except for the diphthongs *ai* and *au*) should be given a pure, continuous sound, as in Italian or Spanish.

Consonants, for convenience, may be pronounced like their equivalents, with the following exceptions:

All aspirate consonants (*kh, gh, ch, jh, ṭh, ḍh, th, dh, ph, bh*) should be pronounced with a strong explosion of breath after the initial consonant. For instance, *ph* is to be pronounced like the *ph* in uphill (though as a single sound), never as an *f*, and, similarly, *th* should be pronounced like the *th* in anthill, never as English *th*.

c is like the *ch* in child. In words of Telugu origin, *c* is pronounced somewhat like English *ts* before a front vowel (*a, ā, u, ū, ŏ, o, ou*). Similarly, in words originally Telugu, *j* is pronounced somewhat like English *dz* before the same front vowels.

ṭ, ṭh, ḍ, ḍh, the nasal *ṇ*, the sibilant *ṣ*, and *ḷ* (which is found only in words of Telugu origin) are retroflex or cerebral sounds not occurring in English and pronounced with the tongue folded back against the roof of the mouth.

ś is like English *sh* but pronounced with the tongue closer to the teeth; *ṣ* may also, for convenience, be pronounced in this way.

r is trilled, as in Spanish or Italian.

For correctness, nonaspirate consonants should not be followed by an expulsion of breath, as the letters would be in English for many word positions.

The nasal *m* may be pronounced as follows:
like *ng* before *k, kh, g*, or *gh* (also written as *ṅ*)
like Spanish *ñ* in señor before *c, ch, j*, or *jh*
with the tongue folded back to the roof of the mouth before *ṭ, ṭh, ḍ*, or *ḍh*
in other situations as an English *m*.

ḥ is a brief echo, preceded by an aspiration, of its preceding vowel.

jñ is approximately *gnya.*

Stress is weaker than in English. In general, the first syllable of a word should have a slight stress, as well as (in Sanskrit words) the next-to-last syllable (penult) if long, or the second-to-last syllable (antepenult) if the next-to-last syllable is short.

Designer: Betty Gee
Compositor: South End Typographics, India
Text: 11/13 Baskerville
Display: Baskerville

www.ingramcontent.com/pod-product-compliance
Lightning Source LLC
Chambersburg PA
CBHW021708230426
43668CB00008B/768
9780520335943